WW II Journals of

Sergeant Frank Pappas

327th Field Artillery

by Dan Pappas

authorHOUSE

AuthorHouse™
1663 Liberty Drive
Bloomington, IN 47403
www.authorhouse.com
Phone: 1 (800) 839-8640

Published by AuthorHouse   09/28/2015

ISBN: 978-1-5049-5047-3 (sc)
ISBN: 978-1-5049-5048-0 (e)

Library of Congress Control Number: 2015915234

Print information available on the last page.

Contents

Dedication

This book is dedicated to the memory of Sgt. Frank Pappas, who served in the 327th Field Artillery Battalion during World War II and to all the men and women who served in the US Armed Forces during World War II. The dedication is to all the men of C Battery of the 327th Field Artillery Battalion of the Eighty-Fourth Infantry Division and all of those who were mentioned in this book. May God bless all of those who never made it back home fighting for our freedom.

Acknowledgments

I wish to thank the following persons for helping me make this book possible. First and foremost, I would like to thank my mom, Diana Pappas, and my father, Frank Pappas, for giving me my grandfather's journals and for helping me figure out the writings in the journals. It would have been impossible without them helping me for endless hours trying to interpret his handwriting and the faded ink and pencil. I would also like to thank my uncle Jim Pappas for giving me all the pictures that he had. Thanks to my uncle Richard Pappas and my wife, Kristina Pappas, for all of their help as well. I could not have done this without my family's support.

Part I

There is a time, or should I say a moment, in a man's life when he relaxes more or less and attempts to recollect certain incidents that directly or indirectly led to his present predicament. Many men, in his short span of living, feels he may have accomplished certain deeds worth remembering or possibly being written of.

I feel such an occasion has made its arrival within me. I write this not to feel proud of myself but only because I should want to remember for always what has occurred during my two years in the army.

The setting for my writing is most appropriate and befitting for you to see. I am now aboard a landing ship tank, bound for France. I have now been aboard five days, protectively anchored within Weymouth Bay along the southern coast of England. As I write this story, I can see most of us are becoming rather impatient, waiting for the seas to calm down so that we may cross the English Channel in the direction of the French coast.

This bit of haven is a most lovely spot, offering us a certain protective seclusion within the war zone. To the north, I can see the small navy base of Portland and at not too far a distance is Weymouth. My eyes travel the shoreline southward, looking to the old sea walls, which have been of great aid in ebbing the rough channel seas from churning us about.

Also in the bay are anchored eleven other landing ship tanks, composing our flotilla, and numbers of other smaller naval crafts. What a target this haven would have been for the Jerries two years ago. Time has passed and with the promise of victory for us and our allies.

I am very much ahead of my story. My intentions were to reveal my thoughts and memories from the very beginning of my induction, and here I am writing of two years hence.

Much has happened in the short span of two years to many of us. And for many of us, our experiences have somewhat differed. It is only natural that we all can't see the same things or recall the same incidents in a similar manner. Some of us are more or less attentive or emotional. As for myself, I should remain neutral, for I don't imagine I can reveal any more than the next man.

I was inducted into the army one year after Pearl Harbor, on December 7, 1942. I also recall the officer in charge remarking, "We can now tell our sons we entered the army on the most historic day of our American history."

Such a remark coming from an officer did not stir me in the least. During my time of writing, never shall I attempt or hint upon any patriotism in my past or any particular enthusiasm for entering the army. I shall be most truthful and frank with myself and those of you who care to read my writings.

Some things in our lives happen in a flash and are easily forgotten with the passing of time. However, such wasn't the case when I left my wife and son for the first time; we didn't know what the future held in store for us. I almost felt my son sensed I was leaving home for some time to come. My wife seemed bewildered and confused, as if not believing or realizing I was leaving. Of course, we understood many families were going through a similar turmoil of confusion. Needless to say, the experience was so new and so unwontedly accepted, we clearly thought only of our grievances, not knowing the future. The hours to follow seemed like a bad dream. Having moments of deep thought, I had hoped time and again that all this was but a bad dream and I soon would be awoken only to be confronted with a cheerful smile from my wife. However, such wasn't the case, for we were now living in this reality.

Never did I realize the occasion would arrive when for the first time in my life I should dislike a train ride. On boarding the train for my new destination, I knew I would be separated from those I love for a long time. Sophie looked lovelier than ever that morning; she was radiantly pretty, as if to look her very best for me only to kiss her good-bye, which was something hard to conceive. My mother, bless her, as hard as she tried, could not help but burst into tears, making it so much more difficult for me to leave.

Our destination was New Cumberland, and we made our arrival there on the morning of December 14. I now was in the army, trying to readjust myself to a new life and a new routine.

My first impression of New Cumberland was to look upon it as a quaint little village. I liked it. Knowing that it was close to home, I felt this would be the ideal place to receive my basic training. However, it was only an induction center, and I knew in a few days I would be transported to a distant camp.

The barracks of North Carolina were warm and comfortable. The two-story building was painted white and reminded me of a secluded country club. It was located on the banks of the Susquehanna, a most beautiful shoreline any season of the year. North Carolina was a community dependent on itself.

It was in North Carolina that for the first time I wore my GI uniform. I will admit I was rather disappointed in my appearance. My uniform did not fit. Somehow I felt a bit of anger. We were constantly on the go while in North Carolina; between gathering supplies and medical examinations, the occasion distracted my attention from home. I resented the attitude of the noncommissioned officers. They appeared to carry on with a certain amount of superiority, which I resented very much. They gave us the bum's rush at every opportune time; however, time has taught we were to do likewise.

We left North Carolina on the night of December 16, never having realized we were to leave that night. The air was cold, blowing in from the north across the icy river to our side of the bank. Walking down the winding roadway leading to our destination, we were faced directly toward the wind. We welcomed the warmth of our makeshift barrack and certainly did feel relieved unloading ourselves of our barracks bags.

In a few moments, we were to start upon a new journey.

I won't say too much about the journey. Everyone seemed to be in a wrapped-up seclusion of his own, thinking of home and those whom he may have left behind. Up until this point, I can't recall the names of any of my new acquaintances. I thought of Sophie and Sonny constantly, wondering how she would manage. Bless her; she did very well. I should have known, though, that she is capable of managing her affairs at home. She has given me little or nothing to worry about. I am more than proud and happy to say she is my wife, for in her, I have found the most important thing in a man's life, and that is a deep devotion and determination within her heart, combined with a willingness to make the very best with the very least.

On the fourth day of our journey, we were to learn we had reached our destination. The morning of December 19 gave us our first glimpse of Camp Howze, Texas. I couldn't believe Howze in the least. It reminded me of an unfinished business venture that had been given up as a total loss. The roads and pathways were ankle-deep in mud. The barracks resembled chicken coops. It was far from my impression of an army camp. I might venture to say that the ensuing nine months did not improve my impression of Howze.

Our basic training commenced on or about January 4, 1943. The weeks to follow were absolutely a new experience. We experienced the coldest winter Texas had endured in the past twenty-five years. Many of the boys contracted the flu during the cold spell. I'd make the acquaintance of a new friend, possibly not see him for several days, and upon inquiring about his whereabouts, would learn he was in the hospital, down with the flu. Days like those were to occur quite frequently in the ensuing few weeks, a bunk to be vacated at least once a day within the battery.

The cadre of noncommissioned officers with a few years of military training to their credit took us under their wings very quickly. The idea was to prove to us that we were now in the army and must forget our civilian past.

They were good soldiers, well trained in their particular techniques. I should always think of Sergeant Hornsby when I think of the army, for in him I found the best all-around soldier in the army. He and I became rather good friends, our friendship lasting until he left for overseas action in Italy. He was a rather unpopular fellow from the start because of his unapproachable attitude [but] later showed his true colors and became one of the boys. As time went by, our training improved, and with that improvement arrived a conventional attitude between the recruits and noncommissioned officers.

We are an artillery battalion, and so our training consisted mostly of command duties pertaining to our positions and, of course, nomenclature, including care and maintenance. Those were bitter and cold days. Sergeant Mann certainly did believe in double-timing us. He must have felt the cold too.

Damn those .30-caliber M1s. Carrying those bastards at right shoulder arms froze the hell out of our fingertips.

One of the coldest nights I ever experienced was the night I was corporal of the guard. I had made corporal only a few days before.

Imbesi told me he couldn't go on any longer. I could hardly blame him for feeling so. He was somewhat of a pest, but I liked him. One glance at him convinced me he was close to exposure, and I knew it was no more than right to have him relieved from post.

Sergeant Lineham and I earned our stripes rather quickly. Lineham and I have been buddies for a long time. He has changed much in the last two years. He seems worried at times.

The completion of basic training means the beginning of field problems and firing practice. With it arrived a much more comfortable change in weather.

In due time, most of us became well acquainted. My close acquaintance included Shirey, O'Neil, Hornsby, Dix, Norceling, Villines, Chumley, Funk, Gabalos, and Werbicki. Each of these names will always bring back a memory either directly or indirectly.

Of course, it wasn't all work and no play. Being away from home meant new foods and a complete change in scenery. I visited cities such as Dallas, Fort Worth, and Denton during weekend passes. Howze in itself was nothing to brag about, but it was centralized for convenience in regard to weekend passes.

Shirey, Hornsby, and Dix have had their ups and downs in the army. Each of these boys had been darn good noncommissioned officers, only to be busted at one time or another, Hornsby and Dix by staff sergeants and Shirey by corporals.

To remember every incident that may have happened in the army is a most difficult thing to do. However, I can say this: never does a dull moment exist. No two days are ever the same. Something new is added with the passing of each day—and with it the accomplishment of an experienced soldier.

Our first field problem was somewhat new to most of us. Sleeping outside was not my idea of comfort. Needless to say, many, many nights were to follow our first night within the next two years—nights under a starry sky, nights under a full moon bright enough to write several letters, nights when we'd put up our pup tents to escape the rain. Yes, night and darkness have played a big part in our training.

To recollect quotations is beyond my mentality. However, I recall Sergeant Hornsby saying, "Pap, a good soldier does not need to know everything. He must have a powerful voice to receive results." I also remember the day Gelson took me into his confidence and said, "Sergeant Pappas, I like you, but I will never go overseas with you, because I'm going to try to get the hell out of this damned army." I wonder how Gelson is. He and I had a lot of fun. Unfortunately for Gelson, he didn't get out, but he was transferred to noncombatant duties.

In the advancement of our training, the time had come when we were to have our first service practice. The old 155mm Schneiders were blockbusters. The boys were willing and determined to know how loud these babies sounded, and so, with this spirit in mind, our executive officer secured the results he had hoped for.

Lieutenant Fay brought us through basic and a greater portion of our future training to come. He was a very informative instructor with a mostly pleasant disposition. Since he was our executive officer, a greater part of our training was under his guidance.

Lieutenant Proctor was then our battery commander. He was a most congenial officer, a man very easy to get along with. We were unfortunate to lose him. The man to take his place was Captain Shaw, a man I never could understand and never cared for.

Many officers have come and gone, some of whom I'd like to meet again and some of whom I don't give a darn if I never see again.

The officers most popular with the boys included Lieutenant Procter, Lieutenant Fay, Lieutenant Clark, Lieutenant Hanson, Captain Robichaux, Lieutenant Staub, Lieutenant Smith, Lieutenant Munson, Lieutenant O'Dell, and Lieutenant Donahue.

I believe the most popular of all the officers is Lieutenant Chrisman. He has been with us many, many months. He built a darn good firing battery that was to eventually take us overseas.

The following weeks of our training included rifle practice at the range. Each new schedule would bring a closer and firmer friendship among the boys. I must not forget the road marches either, for it was there that it would be determined there who was flat-footed and who was not.

Poor Slim Mendenhall, I saw that fellow drag into camp an hour after the battery had returned. I believe his height carried to much weight for his size 15 GI shoes. He stood a mere six feet seven.

We must all have come from Daniel Boone's home state, for there were more expert rifle pins glistening across the chests of the men in the battery than the ordinary eye can catch. The best I could make was marksmanship.

Summer was now nearing, and a ruddy complexion was had by all. The food was never exceptional; however, we did add extra poundage to our weight. Most of us improved much in personal and physical appearance. We developed a taste for nicer and cleaner-cut uniforms. The big improvement was in the fitting of the uniforms—especially in the wearing of the cap. The assurance and cockiness of a good solider are determined in most cases in the manner in which he sets his cap on his head.

We were now soldiers with almost six months of training. An album of memories was already embedded within our minds. We could now look back on a few night problems—to our credit, things were possibly a little scary now and then. We could not have foreseen what would come in the months to follow.

We saw several service practice problems, some successful and some a great disappointment. However, in the coming months, we were to improve very much.

The point I am trying to emphasize is that we now wanted a furlough. A little time at home is such a morale booster, and since this was our first time away from home, the coming furlough was a most welcome venture.

1230
November 16, 1944

Much has happened since I initially began this writing. I am now in Germany. The long-awaited push has begun. The things I have done and the places I have been to within the past few weeks seem like but a dream today. Only the future is a matter of importance in this manmade war.

In a moment of deep thought, a man wonders—what does all this lead up to? Sometimes a bit of radicalism seeps within my confused and doubtful mind. Can it be that the few leaders ruling the world, having control economically and socially and over four billion people, planned for this together? The elements of human nature are allowed only to reach a certain level, and then they are pounded down again below water level.

I can think of several reasons of why this war may have begun. I shouldn't write of them now, and so with a little doubtfulness, I shall continue with the story I first intended to write. Our battery has opened fire, and so for the time being, I shall cease writing. Being ammunition sergeant, I may be called upon at any moment.

I received my first furlough on June 14, 1943. It was disappointingly short. However, the ten days at home were most pleasant. It certainly was tough leaving Sophie and Sonny again.

Being back on the harness meant the beginning of more advanced training. Our problems increased: we were now gaining the experience of full field soldiers. Living in the field three to four days at a time was becoming a habitual routine. Night firing was also added to our training, as did miles of complete-blackout driving.

We were now training harder than ever to prepare for the D Series, which was to last ten days, a preliminary to the Louisiana Maneuvers.

The days were hot and dry, and the roads dustier than ever. To cuss and swear form here to kingdom come was ordinary. Sweat and gum were to play a major part in our training. We learned the importance of artillery the hard way.

Digging in gun emplacements, camouflaging, observing of enemy planes, working in darkness, and learning the art of dispersion all added up to making a good firing battery. Discipline was to determine the success of our outfit.

The D Series had now begun. Accidents were to happen frequently. On the very first day, traveling behind Sergeant Lipperman, I saw his truck upset at the turn. Approaching his upset vehicle, I imagined the worst had happened. Fortunately, the seriousness of the accident was very slight.

The beginning of the series meant the beginning of many sleepless nights. Going into positions and location ammunition dumps was to happen quite often. Driving in blackouts for hours at a time between gun positions and ammunition dumps was to be learned the hard way. And as I mentioned earlier, I was now ammunition sergeant.

Early one morning, the battery moved out very quietly, leaving the entire section, I included, behind. There is a rather good story behind this, but it is much too long to write.

The Diamond Ts were monstrous-looking babies. Joe Werbicki had been my driver, and together we always made a go of it.

The series is now over, and, to the satisfaction of brass hats, was a success. We returned to camp at the end of ten days.

The remaining few weeks prior to the two-month maneuvers served as time to increase our service practice and brush up a little on our past training.

We were now preparing and revaluating ourselves for the coming maneuvers.

Again, it wasn't all work and no play. Shirey, Finehorn, and I were going to Denton frequently. Denton was a typical American town. I knew a place where the food and service was good and usually hitchhiked to town. DiMaio was usually my buddy. Our lunch always held up. A weekend from camp was always a good rest cure. The weekend prior to our leaving was a grand finale to Howze and Texas, and Finehorn and I really celebrated.

We were now ready for the maneuvers. The barracks were emptied. All equipment was packed and stored. After the signal to go, once again we were on the march, only to leave Howze for the last time with an abundance of memories beginning nine months before, some bad and some pleasant.

Many days have gone by since I began this story telling of my days and experience in the army. I do not intend to go any further with my story, for I have seen too much now to make my post an interesting subject. The future is the important thing.

However, I can reveal that we went through two months of maneuvers in the Louisiana swamps, a preparation for what was to follow on the front lines today. Upon completion of maneuvers, we arrived in Camp Claiborne on November 16, 1943. This camp was built during the early days of construction, so it had the necessary conveniences to make a soldier feel comfortable. All of us like this place. Our training there was a repetition of what we had in Howze. Many firing and field problems made up the better part of the training. On several occasions, I visited towns nearby: Shreveport, Alexandria, and Opelousas.

We were called off a field problem, having orders issued to our outfit to make preparations for overseas movement.

The weeks to follow consisted of packing and crating and the issuing of new clothing and equipment. We were now being revolutionized into a combat division. Finally, on September 8, 1944, we boarded troop trains at Claiborne station, our destination a complete secret.

Our trip was a most pleasant one. The morale was very high. The composition was quite noticeable from the trip twenty months before.

On the morning of September 11, we had a twenty-minute stop at the station in North Philadelphia, my hometown. Brother, it was certainly swell to see Philly once again.

In a couple of hours, we arrived at our embarkation point, Camp Kilmer, New Jersey, only an hour ride from Philadelphia. Kilmer was to be our last stopping off point prior to shipment overseas.

On the fourth day of our stay, I received a twenty-four-hour pass to go home. This was the day I had been planning for. Home at last, with Sophie, Sonny, and my mother—a few hours at home meant so much. Sophie was so lovely. We crammed a lifetime into twenty-four hours for we didn't know when we should ever meet again.

Shirey and Ike came over for dinner. My mother and Sophie's mother were also there. When it was time to go, we left without much ceremony and tears. That is exactly how I had hoped it to be. Back at Kilmer, I was disappointed to hear that future passes had been cancelled. We were now alerted and ready to ship out.

My story to date is completed. I wrote at every opportune time, and consequently, the dates are not in order, and journals with many days between events causes a disconnect between events leading to the present day.

However, I've tried to recall my story and possibly make it entertaining. Much has been omitted, such as the conduct and mannerisms of my many friends. I've mentioned only a few of the boys, and they in very minor detail.

Today, we are all overseas, experiencing a much newer life. Our command ship has become ever so much more a place for bonding, for now we are depending on one another for dear life.

Several days after I had begun my initial writing, I felt an urge to keep a day-by-day writing of my experience overseas. The ensuing pages are of incidents and experiences enacted by my friends and myself. I hope to live through this mess. I pray for the day when I can come home again to my dear wife and mother. I want to play with Sonny and enjoy his companionship. I want my family to remember me as in the past.

I am now nearing the climax of the past. Again, I repeat that the dates are confusing, because while writing of the past, I was also writing of the present, which leads up directly to the present day of November 30, 1944.

I shall continue to write at every opportune time, and possibly someday I should read this story to my dear wife. To be in her presence and not have to fear shell bursts and shrapnel is my only desire. May God be with us at all times, to give us strength and courage to face the future, to give us total victory and a climax to this horrible mess.

The past is completed upon these pages, and upon these same pages, with God's help and the answered prayers of my wife and mother, I shall continue to write of the future to come.

We sailed for England on or about September 18, 1944, only to return to New York after colliding with an oil tanker about forty miles out at sea. The weather was very foggy.

The best break we received since being in the army was to return to port. This gave me another chance to go home, and I certainly was glad to be back. I never regretted Camp Kilmer. I had several opportunities to go home. Home is a wonderful world. It gives one the warmth, comfort, and an understanding that is so lacking in the army.

Sophie and I spent a few happy hours together. It certainly was a great surprise to Sophie and my mother to see me return.

On the last morning, when I was to kiss Sophie good-bye, I knew it would be the last time for quite a while. I'm so glad that she brought Sonny to the window. Poor fellow—he was half asleep.

On September 28, we boarded the English vessel *Stirling Castle* (twenty-eight thousand tons) for the second time within a period of less than two weeks. She was patched up and seaworthy once again. The trip across the North Atlantic Ocean was rather calm. We observed blackout regulations throughout. Our convoy consisted of at least forty ships, mostly oil tankers, including one airplane carrier. Accommodations were very crowded; at least five hundred men were on board.

We landed in Liverpool, England, on October 10, 1944 and saw very little of the city. We then proceeded by train to South England. A twelve-hour journey took us to our camp, the most disappointing place we were stationed in since our entry into the army. Two hundred hundred other fellows from the battalion were selected to make up a company of truck drivers and continue onward to France. We became known as the Red Ballers. I was to be a section chief, in charge of forty men.

During my short stay in England, I visited Salisbury, a most picturesque little town only fourteen miles from camp

On the sixth day after our landing, we who are now known as the Red Ballers became somewhat organized, and with our convoy of thirty trucks, we rode to an English Channel port. On the morning of October 16, 1944, we boarded the landing ship tank.

England must be imaginary. It is much too beautiful to be true. The beauty of England is enwrapped in its aging landmarks and beautiful countrysides. The towns are picturesque, quaint, and very old. The rolling hills give one a clear view for miles around. England is enriched with color and harmony. To describe England is as difficult as to describe the beautiful tree of paradise. The pattern is so perfect and so methodically dotted with supremacy of natural beauty. To say that I have seen England in all its beauty would belittle my eagerness. I have seen its beautiful, hilly countrysides only. I have every indication to believe it is very old. There is an understanding and a willingness to help among the English. The developments of their communities reveal so.

October 22, 1944

We have dropped anchor, arriving somewhere along the French coast last night. At the moment we are waiting for the tide to come in so that we may make a landing on the beach.

The crossing of the English Channel was rather rough and choppy. The landing ship tank can't take the terrific pounding of the high seas. A few of the boys become rather seasick during the fourteen hours of our journey.

I've been up on deck for a few minutes. The air is cold. Many ships are anchored a few hundred yards offshore, with transports and freighters making up the greater portion of vessels. I noticed several sunken ships and can see the ravages of destruction along the beach caused during the fury and length of the invasion. One cannot imagine and compare the quietness and stillness of today with what happened almost five months before. We are miles away from the front lines, but there is every indication that the front line had its actual beginning on this very beach.

With twenty-two months of intensive training behind us and an album full of memories, we finally made a landing on the Normandy beach. I see at least six sunken transports about one thousand yards offshore, their masts reminding one of dead trees in the swamps of Louisiana.

October 23, 1944

I am now in France, in the section known to all of us as Normandy. True, the land is lined with miles upon miles of bushy hedge groves. The simple beauty of France lies within its small villages and acres upon acres of apple orchards separated by thick and highly grown hedge groves. The land is rich; the people of France cultivating the land through the centuries have much to be proud of. In all its wreckage, Normandy still stands as a symbol of peace and beauty. The destruction and ravages of war can scar the creations of beauty but shall never make them disappear.

I walked the railroad ties this morning with Sergeant Domanzich and observed a church steeple at a distance. Entering the town, we were greeted by the old folks. Only the too old or too young have remained behind. The youngsters of France are a picture of health. I am amazed of the brightness of color upon their cheeks. Their rosy complexion should make the deep redness of the apples blush with shame.

I picked a flower at the foot of the statue of Saint Theresa as a symbol of protection. I visited the cemetery in the old churchyard and saw many hand-beaded wreaths upon the graves. The faith of Catholicism reigns supreme. Religion has never lost its true meaning here.

October 24, 1944

Rain can be most welcome, but it can be most unwanted and inconvenient at times.

I find it the latter. We have had rain almost continuously for the past several days. Most difficult to do is trying to keep my feet warm. We've been sloshing in mud for some time and have the resemblance of frontline troops. I try to keep dry, but it seems almost impossible.

Our area, before we entered, was a nicely grooved apple orchard. Today, it has taken on the aspects of a bullring or a muddy racetrack.

Going by way of the slushy mud, I paid a second visit to the old village, which is swamped from days of continuous rain.

I made an attempt to speak to several of the inhabitants, but my limited French and their just as limited English helped very little in bringing us to an understanding.

Standing in the old churchyard, I observed down below children playing one of our old familiar childhood games. I thought of Sonny then, for they are not much older than he. I knew I had much to be grateful for, feeling that Sonny, Sophie, and my mother were safe in America. The people here have suffered much. They have lived through a war and know the hardships and destruction that must follow. In all their tragedies and weariness, they still possess the spirit and willingness to face life. For it is people like them who have made France a proud and loving nation.

I haven't any idea when I shall add any more to what I have written. We are a part of the Red Ball supply organization, consisting of fifty GMC trucks and trailers, which are to make up two convoys.

We are prepared to move out in the morning and shall be on the march for some time to come.

October 29, 1944

Much to our surprise and great disappointment, the Red Ball outfit has come to an abrupt and sudden end. The Eighty-Fourth Division artillery received orders to proceed to France immediately, and those of us who left for France two weeks before received orders to rejoin our old outfit, the 327th Field Artillery.

In the short space of time the Red Ballers were on the road, I was fortunate to lead the first convoy on a round-trip journey from Cherbourg to Paris. I rode the leading vehicle, relying mostly on strip maps and French road maps. The convoy consisted of twenty trucks hauling ninety tons of supplies for front line troops. We were on the road forty-four hours, and our route took us through war-torn France, beginning at Cherbourg and leading into the northeastern section of Paris.

I have seen plenty, but the destruction of France is beyond describing.

Saint-Lô, poor Saint-Lô. Destructible Saint-Lô. The fury of war and destruction played havoc upon this little town. Only the name remains. I hardly believe I exaggerate when I say barely a stone or brick remains in its original setting. Saint-Lô is merely a name today, for the original site is a mass of debris.

We traveled through 520 miles of devastation. Towns such as Saint-Lô, Montebourg, Isigny, Carentan, and Argenton form a pathway of destruction leading into Paris.

Upon completion of our trip, we received a rest period at our base camp, which was situated two miles west of Chartres.

I paid a visit to this old town, which was first settled early in the eleventh century, and went to the Chartres Cathedral. I am amazed by the magnificence and beauty of this ancient structure.

One cannot in the matter of a couple of hours capture the full and Gothic beauty of the cathedral. History reveals that as it stands today it was completed in the year of 1260.

To me, it is a huge testament to the ability of the artistic masters of France. The cathedral is a masterpiece of art and ingenuity, combining the pride and patience of a master's wonderful and brilliant mind. I shall always remember the magnificence of this structure, a most beautiful piece of work I had often heard of but had never seen until now.

Traveling the Red Ball highway has shown us that France is a land of destruction.

War has played tragedy and suffering among its people. I wonder if we are to blame. I think of poor Saint-Lô and wonder if the sacrifice wasn't much too large a price to pay. The people of France shall never forget what has befallen them, for there are too many scars to be healed.

November 11, 1944

Today is Armistice Day, a day set aside for those who died in the last war. Instead of hearing prayers of solemnness, I heard artillery fire and airplanes flying overhead.

Upon the disorganizing of the Red Ball, we rejoined the 327th and have now moved up to the front lines. Today is the first opportunity I have had to add anything to my writing.

Much has happened since my last notation.

Our trip began on the outskirts of Saint-Lô, traveling the Red Ball highway, and continued through Paris, arriving there in the early afternoon. Paris and Versailles are places I should like to visit again. It's a most wonderful thrill to travel as an artillery battalion, watching people wave and toss flowers and kisses.

We then traveled through Northern France and into Belgium and Holland. Neither of these countries has suffered much destruction. Towns such as Mons, Liege, and Brussels have hardly been touched. Towns in Belgium look so much like American towns, and I've become rather homesick. We covered more than five hundred miles in our long march, a most difficult march on the wear and tear of our tractors. Vehicles such as those are not built for long trips, and we saw a most terrific strain upon the bogies and tracks.

It rained and snowed throughout the trip. At times it was very cold.

I've received seven letters from Sophie—the first time I've heard from her since I left home on September 28.

We are moving up tonight in a complete blackout. I shall be thinking of those at home. I have been hearing artillery fire continuously. This may be the big push, and if so, may it be short and sweet. I hope the element of Mother Nature doesn't hamper us too much. She has been rather mean lately.

I just heard that the 325th Field Artillery Battalion was attacked and wiped out. It may be only a rumor. I hope so. German planes are flying overhead. The artillery has been spasmodically heavy. We are only twelve miles from the front lines.

November 13, 1944

This is a war of much confusion. We haven't had a chance to clean up for the last three days. The most difficult thing for a soldier to do is keep clean.

We have moved up and are only three thousand yards from the German lines. We are well dug in. This is going to be the long-awaited push. Much depends on the success of this push. I spoke to an officer attached to the Ninth Armor Division who says this is to be more tremendous than D-day.

War is an odd thing. Here I am, deep in the cellar of a German house. We are hoping it proves to be good shelter in case the Germans open up. German homes look typically American. The furniture's the same as what we may find in any American home. The homes in this town have been badly damaged by artillery; however, they can easily be repaired. Nothing I have seen yet can ever compare with Saint-Lô.

The day has come. This is what we have trained for. The ammunition has been brought to position. The guns are dug in. We are now waiting for the zero hour. May God bless us all.

1900
November 14, 1944

We are still waiting for the fireworks to commence.

The hour will arrive; however, it simply must begin very soon, for weather is closing in. Mud and slush still prevail. Snow flurries are falling.

Lieutenant Proctor revealed that if and when the firing begins, 224 guns will participate. What a racket this will make.

I want to live through this, for it is much too near the end to die now.

We have been situated in this German town for the past three days. I never did learn the name of this place. I wonder what may have happened to the families who left these lovely little homes.

What a setup we have. Landry, Long, Lloyd, Ian, Stockton, McQuiston, Martine, Simon, Villines, Boswell, and I have taken over the basement of this German home. We have the comforts of home, though of course in a very crude and primitive manner. But it does provide a roof over our heads, and we did manage to find a little coal stove to keep warm and dry.

The morale is high. It doesn't seem obvious we are so close to battle. Time and patience will tell. McQuiston revealed, "I hope every man in this outfit lives to go home." May his wish come true. We are facing ten German battalions, to my estimation—a very strong force. The Jerries have been tantalizing us now and then with their famous 88 mm.

14

Where are the Royal Air Force and the American Eighth Air Force? I heard much of them back in the States but have yet to see them in mass formation over Germany.

I feel sorry for Corporal Chumley. He is certain to be a father by this time and then there's Chet Nordling who too will soon be a father. Chumley should be giving out the cigars soon. I wish him luck; he may receive word from home soon. The expectancy of fatherhood can certainly age a man in appearance.

2000
November 15, 1944

There seems to be a bit of confusion as to who fired the salvo a few moments ago, the Jerries or us. The walls shook and candlelight flickered. All of us made a dash for the basement.

I've been in the kitchen all evening. Shirey cooked up a stew made up of German ingredients, and we managed to find a bottle of scotch. What a war. What a war. The famous 88s are bursting all around us, but we have a bottle of good scotch to warm us up and good old mulligan stew to boot, with ingredients from German victory gardens. What a war. What a war. The scotch was most certainly welcomed.

British Thirtieth Corps are in air support. Powerful British search lights are flickering their beacons through the dark, misty night. Possibly the infantry is advancing. The Jerries certainly opened up tonight. All's quiet on the Western Front for the time being. Jerry's probably lost his fuse wrench. He fired most of the time directly overhead. His initial date is not far off.

1210
November 16, 1944

The hour has come. The American artillery has opened up. The 240s are sending a barrage over that has no equal. With it has arrived a most lovely day. There is spring in the air. It's the first time the sun has been shining in Germany since our arrival six days ago. The infantry and British and American tanks have been moving forward all morning. The US Air Force has been pounding German lines continuously. The artillery is really going to town now. I hope the firepower is effective. We haven't opened up yet, but when we do, the enemy will send plenty in return. They usually do. They are certain to have our position surveyed and plotted on the map.

Those 240 mm certainly vibrate the elements of earth and sky.

C Battery has opened up. This is not a service practice, so let's make every shot count. Lots of luck.

The evening is still young. The air is chilly; the sky is clear. I think of home often. I wonder what Sophie may be doing.

I should have joined the navy. I gained knowledge of their good setup when I spent six days on board the landing ship tank. Mud, mud, and more mud—I had a good share of it the night the Red Ballers received first load. We tramped in mud for seven hours, resulting in cramps in the legs. Three weeks have gone by, and we are still tramping in mud.

Our artillery has been pounding the German lines continuously for the past two days. Some one thousand prisoners have been taken since we began the attack. Our firepower has been effective. Several towns have been taken by our infantry. Tomorrow shall be a big day for the 327th. We should give them all we have. We may move forward tomorrow night.

One can certainly lose track of the days on the front lines. We have been pounding the hell out of the Jerries for the past fourteen hours. I have seen prisoners coming in. They are certainly a messy lot. I have been busy with the ammo all morning. It takes plenty of beef to handle those shells. I admire my men very much. They have been a great help to me. Landry has been keeping me on the ball. I have some damn good men working with me. Landry, Boyte, McQuiston, and Boswell are really on the ball, as have Lloyd, Ian, Martine, and Long. Every one of these boys has been putting out continuously, hand-handling more than 650 rounds of high explosives.

The artillery is causing much destruction. Reports coming in say our barrage has destroyed a panzer division. Our firepower has been very effective against pillboxes and emplacements.

The night is still. There has been a lull in fire for the past hour. We certainly worked to pass the ammunition today, receiving and distributing ammo until late in the evening.

German bombers dropped a few bombloads very close to our positions.

The enemy artillery has been unusually quiet. They must have taken a terrific pounding from us.

If Hitler has done away with religion, then the people of this town knew nothing of it. In every German home I've entered, I've found Bibles in drawers, saintly pictures hanging on the wall, and saintly statues upon the mantelpieces. Religion is still in existence in Germany.

Man has been taught to kill. Sometimes we wonder if all that we are doing is not entirely wrong. We are told to hate and distrust each other, and yet when I look at a German's home, I think of ours. I see no difference.

November 19, 1944

Today is Sunday, our second Sunday at the front lines. C Battery had been quiet all day. Since coming to this position—or, I should say, since the present drive initiated—C Battery has fired more than four hundred complete rounds. Combined with the entire battalion, that is terrific firepower when concentrated on a certain area.

For the first time, I saw an A20 go down in flames. I'm sure the crew never had a chance to escape. German ack-ack was certainly working on our bombers. In a few moments, we received fire mission to silence those babies. C Battery completed a barrage of forty rounds upon close fire. The mission was accomplished.

Lieutenant Chrisman asked me if I've seen enough action to convince me that we are now at the front lines.

The night is misty. The entire Western Front is ablaze tonight, our artillery firing heavily at intervals.

November 20

Dearest Sophie,

Can you remember the pleasant Sundays we used to spend together? I thought of you constantly today, for there was peace and quiet on this cool and sunny Sunday morning. Much has happened since the day I left you, and no matter how rough conditions will be, I will pull through, for I know and feel that what little I may accomplish here will take me back to you so much sooner.

As I write this note, I can almost sense that you are very close to me. I can so plainly and vividly see you. Only to feel the touch of your arm for a moment would be so heavenly.

I am at the front lines. We are moving up in the morning. I only ask that I come out of this mess safe and sound. Pray for me, dear. I have so much to live for. I want to come back to you and Sonny. You are my future.

Love,
Frank

I am told that I sing in my sleep. For several nights, one of the boys have been hearing singing, but we never could find out who it was—until one morning when Landry came off guard. He awoke several of the boys and said, "Listen to Pappas. He's the one who sings in his sleep." To think that it was I who did the singing was most surprising to me, for I thought it was rather odd for anyone to sing while sleeping. Many times I've been told that I talk in my sleep, but to sing is a new one for me.

November 20, 1944

The angels of war have been kind to us compared to what our infantry have gone through to penetrate deeper into the Siegfried Line.

We have moved three miles deeper into the line. The German fortifications were built to stand terrific firepower.

Never did I dream that someday I would find shelter in a German pillbox on the Siegfried Line. The Jerries left this place in a hurry. I wonder how many of our boys lost their lives to take this pillbox. If I had come down here only five minutes sooner, I would have acquired a German Luger. My men beat me to the punch. Boswell, Bauman, and Werbicki can now boast the ownership of a Luger. Better luck next time.

Much ammunition and firearms were left behind in this pillbox. I did get a German rifle and an ammunition belt with eight pouches of shells and a bayonet.

This fortification resembles a submarine very much. It seems very odd to sleep here, using German bedcovers.

It rains all day. War is entirely a messy job. I've seen many British tanks knocked out by 88 mm while moving forward. I didn't see any dead Germans, only a few livestock, although the dead Germans are scattered in this area.

We have been lucky so far. On each advancement we've made, we have managed good shelter and protection furnished by the heinous. This pillbox is comprised of three sections. The largest is our sleeping quarters. It is about twenty square feet. The Germans had a good and comfortable setup here.

We are a little crowded here, but it is much better than sleeping in a foxhole seeping with water. To reveal who is down here would sound like a roll call. Sergeants Hock, Turner, and Feathers; Corporals Bauman, Pritchard, and Johnson; Privates Boswell, Moolsen, McQuiston, Landry, Davis, Werbicki, and I, we are the fortunate soldiers of fortune making this place our home for the time being.

If I had been in the infantry, no doubt I never would have written about my experiences of the past few weeks. I wonder what my next shelter will hold in store for me. According to the law of averages, I am about due for a foxhole.

May Hitler live in peace and may peace bring him hell.

November 21, 1944

How in the world our doughboys ever took over this line is beyond me. In the two days that I've spent in this new position, I have closely observed the construction of these pillboxes. By the way, the engineers came through today and gave orders to blow up all pillboxes, and so I am now without shelter. The pillbox won't be dynamited until we advance again, and I've made this place my shelter for the time being. Landry and I started our emplacement, but it became too dark to continue. These pillboxes are constructed of steel and concrete at least two feet thick. I saw our pillbox blown to bits with 650 pounds of TNT. One of the doors weighing at least three hundred pounds was blown sky-high, landing only five feet from my tractor.

I had a good scare this morning while unloading some ammo. Six Messerschmitts swooped down upon us. I thought my time had come. This was the first time since coming to the European Theater of Operations that I really hit the dirt.

I've observed much German equipment, including clothing, blown to bits, strewn in the potato patches. Germans paid dearly here at the hands of our artillery. Behind us lie Geilenkirchen badly damaged by our artillery. She was our objective from the beginning of this drive. I have seen much gruesomeness that is not too pleasant to reveal. War is horrible. We must kill or be killed. Our infantry show no mercy. 333rd have orders to kill every German, and they have been following orders. British say our men are the toughest they have yet encountered. The Ninth Army is on the go, the Eighty-Fourth is on the go, and the 327th is on the go. I hope General Simpson and General Eisenhower know what they are doing. I can't see peace being so near for a long time to come.

November 23, 1944

Today is Thanksgiving. Considering some of the narrow escapes we'd had, we are all thankful to be alive.

I wonder what it is like to sit at a table and enjoy a fine meal. It seems like ages since I sat at a table with Mom, Sophie, Sonny, and Joe. I haven't had a good bath since I arrived here. I've been on the front lines for almost two weeks. Pieces of shrapnel and concrete have hit the ground next to me many times in the past couple of days. Jerries put up a counterbattery attack yesterday. Shells were whizzing by in all direction.

Reports coming from the infantry say our casualties are heavy. We may be winning the war, but we are paying a heavy price. We haven't bogged down yet, but when our guns do, there will be hell to pay.

I went down to Geilenkirchen today. I combed through several buildings, looking for a pair of boots—no luck. Making this town our new quarters, the entire fifth section has taken over a basement under the railroad station. This town was still a hot spot for German artillery. I hit the ground twice today and once yesterday. I certainly dread shrapnel.

Rain, rain, and more rain—and not to mention the mud. I'm inclined to believe heavy artillery fire has quite a bit to do with atmospheric pressure. Where there's war, rain surely will follow. The weather has been rough on all of us. I've been wet to the skin for the past three days, but I finally had the chance to dry up and bathe in our new home. This place could be a lot better, but I know of places that are much, much rougher. Yes, today is Thanksgiving in Geilenkirchen. She can only be thankful in that firing as stopped in her charred and destructed homes. This is war at its greatest strength. By golly, today is my birthday. What in the world ever made me think of my birthday is beyond me. A man has so much more important things to think of—for instance, the chance to live and survive.

November 24, 1944

Shells bursting close by are far from soothing music. A nice thought at a time like this is to think of home, your wife, your mother, your son—thoughts that are an impossibility but a great help to morale.

The new campaign has not been favorable. The 334th Infantry have taken a horrific pounding. They have fought too well, taking their objectives. Consequently, the losses have been heavy. German prisoners admit the Eighty-Fourth Division is the toughest outfit they have yet encountered either here or on the Russian Front.

German artillery has been bursting close to our position for some time. They are very poor artillerymen. I certainly pray a direct hit doesn't hit us. If one does, I can only account at this moment that it was a lucky shot. May they continue to miss, for I shall never know I had lived if a direct hit happened. I had no sooner completed the last sentence when we thought this place was going to crumble from three shells bursting.

God be with us. Sophie, you'll never know how many times you come close to being a widow.

November 26, 1944

The weather has been wonderful today. I hope it continues to be. We then may make some headway. Germans counterattacked yesterday; however, we held our ground. At one time, we were told German tanks had penetrated our sector of the line. We're still waiting for reinforcements. Artillery fire has been light today. Germans have been shooting more than we have. Geilenkirchen still seems to be an occasional target for the Germans. I cross the railroad tracks several times a day, and in doing so, I often wonder when the next shell will land. Many have landed, but luckily, I wasn't there at the time. Casualties in artillery personnel are relatively small; however, there is always a first and last time. I've learned mighty fast how to hit the dirt in a split second. Being a civilian must be wonderful: no bombs, shells, or snipers to fear—no mud, rain, or wet, stinking clothes to contend with. Yes, it must be wonderful to be a civilian, but I'm not ashamed to say that I am a dirty GI. For it takes dirty GIs like Dix, Farina, Robisk, Finehorn, and dozens of others to make democracy safe for the playboys back home.

I'm tired, but I can't rest. I can't think into the future, for it appears so hazy and undetermined. I can think only into the past, and in my thoughts of the past, I see my mother, a most wonderful little woman upon whose lap I laid my sleepy head many a night and slumbered into a peaceful coma.

At times, I wonder if I have left behind a memories bouquet in my mother's memory album. Does she recall my childhood days as vividly as I? Has she been proud to say that I was her son? I can't be too sure that in me she found a son she had hoped for. Memories are so many when you think of your loved ones. I want my mother to be proud of me, but I wonder if I failed her. Yes, a time arrives in a man's life when he only lives in the past, for it was in the past that he found happiness and contentment. My mother, my father, Sophie, Sonny, Abe, Joe—they all fit into the making and the pattern of my life. My friends Eddie, Dalina, Joe Fantasia, Bucky, Johnny Soto, Johnny Zizoo, Fishy, and so many others come back to me after these many years. Many of them are in the armed services today, some, I included, fighting at the front lines today.

On our fourteenth day on the front lines, my thoughts go back to the very first time I ever kissed Sophie. Sweet girl—she recalls our courtship very much more vividly than I. The long walks in the park, her favorite songs, holding hands in the movies, window shopping, occasional parties and dances—unimportant as they may seem, it is memories such as these that webbed a linking tie in our lives to bring a mutual understanding and a deep devotion to our marriage. June 21, 1941, is a day I shall never want to forget. Sonny, a dear little fellow with whom I've spent very little time is the pride and joy of my mother. I pray that in him she shall find the love and tenderness she had so wantonly wished for in me.

In true reality, memories of the past aren't entirely pleasant. I shall never forget the look upon my mother's face, the tears in her eyes, or the anguish in her heart during the Depression days when she had lost all. In all her grievances, she has never been defeated, for in her heart, she is determined to face the realities of living. May God, always be close by to protect her, for it is she who has suffered and sacrificed for my upbringing and welfare.

And for Sophie, too, memories weren't entirely pleasant. I've caused her to shed tears many times. Youth is a wonderful possession; however, at times, it is invisibly imposed. And at such times as these, I unthinkingly and stupidly caused conflict and sorrows in dear Sophie's heart. Sweet little girl, I love you dearly.

I have been rather tired lately, mentally and physically. The time is now 2:20 a.m. We received a message over the phone that Germans are infiltrating our lines disguised as American soldiers.

Activity has been very quiet these last three days. Another drive will begin very shortly. Supplies and ammunition are coming in. The H hour is contemplated to be sometime late this afternoon.

We are lucky so far. God must be with us. Though many shells have zoomed by our positions, we haven't yet had a casualty. May it continue to be this way.

A full moon casts its shadow over war-torn Germany. At one thirty this morning, I looked about. The air was still. The extreme brightness of the moon threw a silvery gleam upon the stars. The elements of Mother Nature cast an exotic and mysterious blend of beauty upon shattered and torn-down Geilenkirchen, as if to weep over or possibly attempt to enliven its former pride of possessive beauty.

Today is our eleventh day in the Geilenkirchen sector and our eighteenth day on the frontlines. Our progress toward Cologne has been very slow. German resistance is very strong and determined. At one point, we were twenty-three miles from Cologne, making our initial advance only seven miles since beginning the drive toward the Rhine River eighteen days ago.

People at home look upon battles of war as something glamorous. If only they could see or know the truth.

A man can die on the field of battle in the same grotesque and gruesome manner as the Germans. Our tanks and weapons are shattered to oblivion and obscurity as much as the Germans' are. We are fighting an enemy who is as determined as we are, an enemy who is evenly matched man for man, gun for gun, and tank for tank. We are fighting a warring nation, a nation who compels us to pay a heavy price in men and material.

Today has been a sorrowful day for C Battery. Shrapnel, the thing we dread the most, caused four casualties.

Miguel, Farina, Hewitt, and Dodgen have earned Purple Hearts in the line of action. The wounds inflicted were serious injuries, with Miguel's injuries possibly being the most serious. He lost three fingers and has also incurred wounds on the stomach and leg. Hewitt was gashed about the face, and shrapnel hit the lower part of his leg. Farina and Dodgen received minor injuries. I sincerely wish this is the last time I will make a notation such as this. It could have been so much more serious. Let's not have any more such occurrences in C Battery.

Tonight we rode in complete blackout to and from the ammo depot. Ordinarily, we have been going after ammo in the daylight. Darkness comes quickly, and with it arrives an alertness of body and mind.

December 1, 1944

GI Funk added 10 years to my age. At two o'clock this morning, he rushed into our dugout, excitedly saying he needed help, that several shells had hit the kitchen and set a fire and that Boswell and Chaney were badly hurt.

Baumon, Werbicki, Doc, and I rushed over to offer help. I imagined the worst had happened. The railroad tracks are a hotbed for shells, and we had to cross them to reach the kitchen. Upon rounding the courtyard leading to the kitchen, we were met by gunfire. I thought surely we were being ambushed by Germans. However, such wasn't the case. A jeep, not the kitchen, was on fire, and possibly ball ammo was in the jeep, thus accounting for the gunfire. Both Boswell and Chaney were badly hurt. Shrapnel plastered the whole side of the building. We've had six casualties in one day. Our position had been shelled upon continuously all day.

B Battery had one truck blown to pieces, and one of ours was riddled with shrapnel.

Coming back from the ammo dump this afternoon, we were caught in the middle of antiaircraft fire, a German Messerschmitt, and machine-gun fire. God, I don't know if our fears are exaggerated, but we have had some close calls. Werbicki, Boyte, and I dismantled the vehicle and squeezed into a one-man foxhole to escape machine-gun fire. Landry, Bauman, and DiMaio, a few yards ahead of us, came to a halt and took cover by the trees. We were, to be truthful, scared at the time, and when it was over, we laughed, remembering how silly we must have looked. Facing death is not my idea of fun, especially when you are fighting an enemy whom you can't see but only hear. Yes, today has been an exciting day for us.

When will the day arrive when a man can look into the sky and have no fear?

December 3, 1944

The time is 0330. Everything is quiet except for an occasional shell burst in the distance. Landry and I are the only ones awake in the basement. This shelter certainly has proven its value in protecting us from artillery fire. We may move forward within the next day or so. We're going for a load of ammo at the break of dawn. I'm sorry to have lost Boswell. He gave me his Luger to hold until he gets back; however, I doubt very much if he will ever return. To me, his leg looked badly shattered at the knee. I hope he is in the States by Christmas, a place where every American soldier had hoped to be this year.

Today is our twenty-second day on the front lines. Everything is unusually quiet along our entire sector. Rumor has it—and the general impression seems to be—that peace terms may be in the making. To me, this is very hard to conceive.

Unfortunately, Chaney and Dodgen died from their wounds. Chaney never regained consciousness from the time I last saw him to the time he reached the hospital. He died en route. Dodgen died sometime yesterday. This is war. We can merely shake our heads; show a little sympathy, think of the good things they did, and go about our duties, quickly forgetting about them and their good deeds.

We are at a complete standstill here. Things are not going along as well as we'd like to in the British sector. The Eighty-Fourth is playing a holding-down position, firing only at counterattacks, waiting for the British to come up on our left flank. German artillery has been light. At times, they will inflict harassing fire, hoping to cause some casualties.

It is not a wise thought to wonder: if we hit the dirt fast, someday, if we are fortunate, we might rejoin our families in a happy celebration of thankfulness.

Part II

The time is 0130. This is the quietest of all nights. When we first occupied position in the Geilenkirchen sector, the enemy was only three-quarters of a mile away from our batteries, and now, sixteen days later, they have retreated to points only about six or seven miles away from us. We have an extreme shortage of ammo. What is going on at the home front? This war isn't over. Give us the ammo. We need it.

0200
December 6, 1944

Dearest Sophie,

I'm thinking of you and also of the last letter I wrote to you. You may be hurt when you read this letter, dear. My intentions were not to write that letter in a manner that could hurt your feelings, darling. I just wouldn't dare be mean to you deliberately.

I was only trying to emphasize to you how important time is here. Everything here depends on time. Time lost is time never regained. Our lives depend on time. The things we accomplish depend on time. My days on this front may be timed, and what little I can spare, I certainly want to share it with you in my heart. A picture of you before me, a new one, a picture I had never seen—for you see, dear, it is possible that we may never meet again.

The closest I can be to you now is by means of a photograph. This is what I wanted to tell you but didn't. My darling, I love you with all my heart and soul. To feel the warmth of your lips upon mine is my desire. Please believe in me, dear. I adore you.

Yours Forever,
Frank

0220
December 6, 1944

Dear Sonny,

Hello, son. How are you? Mommy tells me how handsome you are. To me, you both make a wonderful and lovely picture. Sometimes I laugh and sometimes I shed a little tear when Mommy tells me you kiss my picture every night and say, "Daddy went bye-bye." Daddy will come back to you and Mommy someday. Be a good boy and look after Mommy. I love you, son, and we both love Mommy.

Daddy

German artillery must have consolidated and dug in new positions east of the Roer River. This morning, for the first time in the last thirty-six hours, 88s landed near our position. Holding our position and line has given us a temporary rest break. Our artillery has been very light these last few days.

It doesn't pay to roam around unnecessarily. We never know when an enemy shell will burst nearby. We have been staying in the basement as much as possible. The morale of the boys is very high. The casualties suffered several days ago has given every indication to all of us that this is war in all its realities, and the lowering of morale is not going to bring it to a quick and final victory.

December 9, 1944

The time is 0230. I wonder what is going on. The entire sector of the Ninth Army has been very quiet for the past three days. The big drive definitely did not materialize as we had anticipated.

One of two things is happening. Either peace terms are being negotiated, or we are waiting for larger quantities of supplies to come up from the rear echelon. Our ammunition supply has been reduced to such an extent that we have been given strict orders from Supreme Headquarters Allied Expeditionary Force to fire only in very critical emergencies.

Doughboys often say we are a gift from heaven when things become rough in no-man's-land. To hear our artillery zooming and whirring over their heads means a blanket of protection and an opening of the way for newer and further advances. After twenty-eight days on the front lines, there is still no indication of a rest period—and to think, war workers back home are promised more bonuses if they continue on with their jobs.

The lull in battle is becoming very monotonous. If days such as these are to continue much longer, this war will go on indefinitely. I'm sure during this lull the Jerries are reorganizing and preparing bigger and better defensive lines. Time means so much. Time determines defeat or victory, life or death—and, yes, sorrow or happiness. Time means so much, even if it be but a minute.

December 11, 1944

Here we are at a complete standstill. There are no signs or indications that we will be taken off the lines. Our guns and tractors have felt the wear and tear of warfare and can have a good going over in our care and maintenance.

We went to the rear lines yesterday for a twelve-hour rest. On the way to the rear, we saw many pillboxes situated at strong and strategic points.

Haarlem is a quiet little town in Holland. A good place to rest and relax, and even if only for a few hours, it is nice to be away from artillery fire for a while. The Dutch have greeted us cordially.

The British have not been dealing too well with the enemy. They will need our support. We are supplying a new offensive, but of course, whenever a drive is successful, the British will get the credit, as usual.

I feel we are fighting the wrong people. We have been led to believe in propaganda that, to my ways of thinking, is no basic truth. We can believe in certain ideals, and yet they don't necessarily have to be true facts. I hate to confess myself as being a fanatic or radical. However, I also believe we are a majority overruled by a powerful minority.

Sergeant Mann thinks on these front lines. He sees the planning and strategic moves that could have been possible. He sees a plan muffed out by the minority, leading to our present predicament.

Politics has played a big part in our world affairs. It will play a big part in the end of this war, because it played a big part in the start of this war. Guns and tanks will not bring victory; a pen and a sheet of paper will decide our destiny. Wars are not won on the field of battle. Wars are won at a conference table.

The majority throughout the world must unite, for it is only in a united world that we shall find permanent peace.

December 12, 1944

We have been on the front lines thirty-two days. In that period of time, the Fifth Section has handled and supplied the gun sections with 2,400 rolls of high explosives approximating a weight of 125 tons.

Here's a nice thought, although it may be too farfetched.

You're sitting at the dinner table with your wife, enjoying a favorite meal she has cooked for you especially. It may be fried chicken smothered with mushroom sauce or a salad decorated with olives and sardines. You look across the table and stare at your wife for a few moments. Her hair is fixed so that it drapes over her shoulders. She looks young and refreshing in her chic and short gingham. The sweet fresh air blowing in through the window brings a scent of complete purity and peace of body and mind. In the sweet scent your wife leaves behind as she passes you by to go to the refrigerator and the freshness and peaceful atmosphere of the kitchen, you reach for your wife, bringing her close to you and kissing her on the lips, her cheeks, her hands. You talk. You whisper. You joke. You long for the future and talk of the past.

Being married to a wonderful and cheerful little girl is so much fun. I know, for Sophie has given me that firm conviction in believing in the future. I will see her again and hear her wonderful voice—a dream so wonderful, a dream so beautiful, a dream come true.

December 16, 1944

For the past four days, we have been standing by, waiting to attack. On several occasions, we've had orders to stand by, only to have the attack postponed to a later date. This waiting and prolonging is helping the enemies to dig in well east of the river. What in the hell goes on around here? We gave the enemies all the time in the world to put up a strong defensive battle. The Jerries have been shelling the hell out of us today. Are we fighting to bring this war to an end, or are we fighting to satisfy the curiosity of a few politicians?

I will admit we haven't had it too bad in this position. There are plenty of rabbits and potatoes to eat. We keep our place comfortably warm. Our beds are soft, and the stories fly thick and fast.

Freezing weather has set in. The ground is hard. Maneuverability is becoming more of a possibility.

Here are some thoughts as I linger on.

The time we'll say is five in the evening. People are rushing, making a dash for the transits. The air is cold and dry. The nostalgic atmosphere of fir trees, the jingling of bells and the colorfully decorated wreaths remind one of the nearing Christmas holidays. The spirit is high and lively. Joy and goodness fill the air. One enjoys living, for everyone is happy.

You arrive close to home with peace in your heart and an arm full of bundles. You approach the steps, and the soft lights in the parlor glimmer a soft tone of peace, warmth, and contentment. You enter, taking a deep breath of warmth and security, for you are now at home—home, sweet home, where doorways give you confidence and a welcome of faith, trust, and the understanding of love and companionship.

December 18, 1944

Linton
Fae
Chet
Moc
Dick

It is names such as these which represent the American army.

When I first began writing of my experiences, I had wished that never would I have to make any entries of casualties.

Once again, the Jerries let loose a barrage of hell and fire, killing three of our men. Captain Chelson and McColsin and a third fellow, a new replacement in our outfit, never knew what hit them. Our position and area have been taken a pounding. We must move to an alternate position.

I received four packages at the most inopportune time. The morale in general is very low. Ordinarily, under normal conditions, these packages would have been most enjoyable, but now it seems that we try to finish everything in one day, for we never know if we shall live through the next day. War is hell.

2115
December 20, 1944

We've been anticipating a drive for the past two weeks, and what happened? Jerry counterattacks and zeros in our position. And so tonight we spend our first night in our new position. My nerves are just about shattered. In fact, most of us are a little on edge. We have been taking a shellacking in counterbattery firing.

Landry, Werbicki, and I have dug our foxhole. Last night we were in the basement of railroad station, and tonight we are in a foxhole in the open field.

Landry and Werbicki have always been good company. There's never a dull moment with them. The three of us have handled the hard move together. May we continue to do so.

If Jennie, Sophie, and Bernice could only see us tonight! I wonder if they realize what we must go through. Joe has his Jennie, Landry has his Bernice, and I have my Sophie. The names of these girls give us the courage and a will to continue. Damn Hitler and all that he stands for.

December 23, 1944

All of us have gone through hell for the past three days. Today has been very calm compared to the past three days. We hadn't shaved or bathed and look like hell.

We are now attached to the First Army. A breakthrough has been made by the Germans in the sector. The Eighty-Fourth traveled more than one hundred miles. We are now in southern Belgium coming in as reinforcement to First Army.

The ammo certainly was a mess. I still don't realize how we ever managed to carry 650 complete rounds of ammo. Tractors and trucks were piled sky-high with ammo and personnel equipment.

Once again Landry, Werbicki, and I have dug a dugout, the second within the past three days. Everybody has slept very little, and everybody has worked hard. Captain Bonel was struck by a half tractor. On the way to sick bay we stopped for the night to sleep. Very little sleep could be had. The night was cold and wet. A robot bomb landed very close to us. We saw the darn thing come over and crash about two hundred yards away from us. Boy, did we hit the dirt. Major Antocheck certainly was a wreck. We all live in suspense. We feel that we are lucky if we can survive from one day to the next.

We have been catching hell physically and mentally. To think that tomorrow is Christmas Eve, and here we are, sitting on the hottest spot on the entire Western Front. May God be with us. May he listen to the prayers from our loved ones, and may he answer them with the greatest of fulfillment.

December 24, 1944

Tonight is Christmas Eve. To us, it is just another night consisting of artillery and mortar fire. Our position is bad. We are in a tight spot. We had orders to stand by to withdraw to a new position.

We saw at least one thousand bombers and escorts fly over us this afternoon. A couple of bombers went down in flames. Dogfights were few.

Our mail service must be out. We haven't received mail for a few days. I haven't had a chance to write any either.

This is a lovely night to be home.

I'm thinking of my family. Yes, tonight is Christmas Eve, and yet we have so little to look forward to.

December 25, 1944

Today is Christmas. I am thankful to be alive and observe another day of the birth of our Lord. So many times in the past few weeks I felt I should never see another Christmas Day. I thought of Sophie constantly today. Hoping to find a clearer mind to think of those close to me, I went to the village church. I found peace and contentment and a new hope. I found confidence and serenity to look forward to spending next Christmas with my family.

Our position is very fluid. We are surrounded. Our artillery has been firing continuously for the past thirty-six hours.

The spirit of Christmas is in our hearts. The spirit to live is within our hearts. The thought and the love of our families are within our hearts, but the shelling must go on if we are to survive and make our hopes and wishes come true.

Today, in war, we observed Christmas in the very best manner with the people of Belgium. May they and God look upon us and make our prayers and wishes a reality.

2330
December 25, 1944

Landry and I just came off guard. The hour and twenty minutes went by rather quickly.

The firepower we have been throwing out for the past three hours is terrific. I can't see how anyone in its path could survive. Everything is getting close tonight, from 105s and 155s to 430s. The fire power we used at Geilenkirchen can't compare with this. The rumbling of artillery is deafening and is giving hell.

December 26, 1944

Four days have gone by, and we still occupy our same position. This is a hilly country. We have plenty of defilade. In between this extreme defoliation we have plenty of hidden firepower consisting of 240s, 155s, 105s, and 4.5s. This sector of the northern front with the First Army may decide the war. We are in a sector that had not felt the scars and destruction of warfare. It is good to smell the fresh air of the valley. The stench of the dead and the gasping odor of chlorate is a most depressing sensation.

0210
December 29, 1944

I have been too tense to add any particulars during the past three days. Our lines are more or less secure now. We have been firing but not as heavily as we did the first three days in position. Reports coming in from the lines say our artillery fire has been very effective. We have broken the German offensive, possibly only temporarily. The morale is rather high. Everyone is in good spirits. Mist and snow have prevailed for the past twenty-four hours.

I held a long discussion with Lieutenant Ramsing on world politics. At last I have met someone of intelligence who sees this messy affair in the same manner as I. We need more men like him—men who can think for themselves, men who can ponder and debate an issue. We must seek and find the truth. We can believe in so many things, and yet they may not necessarily be the truth. We must know the truth. We must find the truth. Theories are not substantial enough to rely upon.

January 3, 1945

This is my first entry for the New Year. Not much has happened in this sector for the past week. The German breakthrough has been checked. I haven't heard an 80 since we left Geilenkirchen.

The British artillery outfit moved near our position today. They are only about one hundred yards from our dugouts. We are moving out in the morning and taking new positions closer to enemy lines. We are now firing at about fourteen hundred yards. The British have no night discipline. They yell and shout and ensure fire missions with a loud speaker, while we use phones. Americans work very quietly in the dark.

I'll now write little about the dugouts. We have been making accommodations for the fifth section. Landry, Werbicki, and I dug a pretty good emplacement. It isn't deep enough, because we struck water. It is about six feet square, and with our little stove, we do manage to keep warm. We walk around more freely in this sector than ever before and have had very little counterbattery fire. A robot bomb huffed, puffed, sputtered, and stalled directly over our dugouts last night. Damn those robot bombs. We have seen a few robot bombs go by our flanks. This is the first to fly directly overhead.

0100
January 4, 1945

We fight the elements of the weather as well as the Germans. Tonight we are in our new position. We have moved twenty miles to help support two armored divisions that are attacking the Germans at the gap, the point where the Germans initially made their breakthrough. The roads were very bad. Our vehicles had very little traction and went as they pleased. Many times we slid to the wrong side.

A Belgian family was nice enough to welcome us into their home. My section and I have taken the second floor. It isn't a very good construction; however, it is a house, and it is good to be in a house once again. Cellars and dugouts do become tiresome, although they are very good protection. Every time our artillery opens up, the old house shakes and vibrates like an earthquake is occurring. We are close to the guns.

This family consists of an elderly couple and their young daughter and grandchild. The son-in-law has been in a German prison camp for the past fourteen months.

Everyone except Landry and me is asleep. The night is very cold and pitch-dark. The wind is howling. This would be a lovely night to hear the Germans have surrendered.

January 5, 1945

Today has been a rough day for everyone. We moved out again, this time advancing four miles. Waking up with the dawn, we found Belgium blanketed in a virgin blanket of white. It snowed all day. Moving to our new position was rough and tedious. On the way, our battery was disabled due to a steep incline, and we couldn't move. Werbicki—good old reliable Werbicki—had to come to the rescue. What would they do without the fifth section? While writing, I saw an American mine blow up, injuring two men. The highway was very slippery and congested.

Our new position is in the hills of Belgium. A chateau serves as our sleeping quarters. The snow is beautiful. We are enveloped by high, steep hills covered with virgin snow. This chateau, or castle, is a beautiful place. It must've cost a fortune to build. However, tonight, Bauman, Landry, Mock, Dick, Campbell, Boyte, Bell, and I are not spending the night at our new position. We are now back at our former one, having returned to pick up seventy-five rounds. The roads are too slippery and dangerous to make the return trip at night. We are to have shelter with a Belgian family for the night. We would have stayed with the family we were with the night before, but there is no place to park the tractor and trucks.

As long as the people of Belgium remain, we can always find shelter and warmth.

January 7, 1945

The scenery on the front lines is beautiful. High on the hill, looking out the window of the chateau toward the south, I see the valley rising to extreme heights and know that only a mile or so on the other side of these steep hills, the enemy is fighting a desperate battle.

The morning is gray and misty, possibly a good indication of more snow. The winding roads lined with tall, rich fir trees and thick shrubs on both sides make one feel so small and unimportant.

This chateau isn't very old; however, it possesses an air of royalty and aristocracy of years gone by. As for myself, I will settle for my little apartment anytime. This place is much too immense to be called home.

The spires and domes stand out as the predominate figure, as if resentful of the occupation of our soldiers. The country once gave one the feeling that in former years there was much gayety and activity. The bleakness of the outside walls somehow gives me the feeling of resentment and uninviting attention.

January 7, 1945

We have been on the front lines for fifty-six days. We of the Eighty-Fourth have fought in too many battles. In the battle of the Rhine Valley, our objective was Cologne on the Rhine. However, this venture proved to be unsuccessful, and now we face the Battle of the Bulge. This last battle is slow and hazardous. The elements of Mother Nature are our biggest hardship.

I have great respect for the Eighty-Fourth Division. We have done well on the front lines.

Our casualties have been heavy and our replacements many; nevertheless, it is still the Eighty-Fourth Division.

Sophie may wear my insignias and feel somewhat proud of our accomplishments. The Germans are amazed. They say we are Frank Roosevelt's special storm troopers. Our infantry and artillery rate with the very best. Individually, we are small and insignificant, but as a whole, we are a good team.

January 8, 1945

My forecasting of more snow was correct. Snow began to fall at six last night, and twenty-four hours later, it's still snowing. This damn chateau is a cold place standing on the high hill.

Since coming to this position, C Battery has fired more than three hundred rounds. Supposedly, the forces of the First Army are to meet the forces of the Third Army. This has been a slow, hard battle. The deep snow may delay our attacks. We are situated in the Ardennes mountain chain, ranging to a height of at least fifteen hundred feet. I wish I could capture the full beauty of the scenery. The countryside looks so full and enchanted, and to think that very section is the battlefront! War demands horror and destruction; however, it is a great consolation to see a gorgeous landscape in all its natural beauty. Momentarily, the wonders of Mother Nature help one to forget wars and the devastation of hard-fought battles.

January 9, 1945

Everything has been mostly quiet today. We moved out of the chateau. For the first time, today the Eighty-Fourth has been mentioned by *Stars and Stripes* as being on the front lines. It's about time. Burchfield received a Purple Heart for a slight shrapnel wound. Reports coming in appear to be favorable. We may advance within the next two days. We have fought almost continuously coming to the position and have been supplying the guns with ammunition at all hours of the day.

The snow is at least a foot deep. Snowdrifts will make some places impassible.

I am now in the kitchen of the chateau. It is nice and warm down here. It is a very large room, and one can find me and many more down here at every opportune time.

January 11, 1945

Of all the damn times to move out. We received our order at four in the afternoon and never did get into position until about eight last night. Yesterday certainly was a rugged day. Every gun had to be winched out of position onto the road. Without the engineer and global navigation chart, we would have never got out. We had a close call with a minefield. We advanced four miles, and it took us five hours to make so short a trip.

I observed many dead humans frozen into the snow. American tanks and German 88s were strewn all over the battlefield. We are now within the mouth of the gap where the Germans initially broke through.

The court's chateau was spared, but the little village near our new position was blown to kingdom come. I went inside of what was left of the village church. Every spiritual statue and crucifix was completely destroyed. Germans are still to be found in the village. The Battle of the Bulge is devastating, and war is hell.

How much more can the ordinary man take? We of the artillery are indirectly the cause of many horrible deaths and tragedies. Being a mile or so to the rear, we are not eyewitnesses to the actual killing, but when we advance up, we can plainly see the havoc we have thrown.

Tonight we are in another dugout. This one was probably dug by Germans. Landry, Bill, and I are the occupants.

This is our sixth position since coming to the front lines.

Men fight for a cause, fighting against the hard and the wicked. We endure hardships that no individual can endure. We pull in, in the dark, unloading ammo under artillery fire. We contend with rain, mud, sleet, snow, and ice. We sleep in cellars, foxholes, and dugouts. We eat meager rations hurriedly, shivering in the cold. We don't bother to change clothes for days or weeks at a time. We live like beasts, hunting, observing, and killing the enemy. Men are such fools and stupid individuals.

January 13, 1945

Today we must have created somewhat of a history in artillery. C Battery was the only battery of the battalion in position to fire, with only twenty-four men to move the guns, handle the ammo, and execute fire missions at the post. We managed to fire more than four hundred complete rounds. We really put them out. At one time, I handled the phone, then Landry rammed in the projectile, and to load, Landry, Campbell, McQuiston, and I loaded and unloaded. B Battery too completed rounds. C Battery really worked and put out in those two hours.

January 15, 1945

The morning is somewhat clear. The sun is shining. Today is our fifth day in this position. The last two have been relatively very quiet. The first two days here we fired close to six hundred complete rounds. We played hell with retreating Germans.

The countrysides are still blanketed in snow. The remains of a few American tanks are still visible. This area or sector was a suicide trap for our tanks. Coming over the hill, they made perfect targets for the German artillery. Many dead Germans are to be found.

The Eighty-Fourth can be proud of its achievements. They fought hard and well.

We thought a German plane had spotted our position the night before last. It flew over us at a low altitude for over an hour. Luckily, it didn't drop any bombs.

On the fifteenth, we received orders that this position was to be our rest camp. It may just as well be, because we fought for the area. We were on the front lines sixty-four days. During this period, we fought in Germany for thirty-one days and from there proceeded to withstand the enemy breakthrough at the Bulge. We were in this battle thirty-three days. We haven't done much for the past three days. The battle line is now about fifteen or twenty minutes away. The Germans withdrew quickly when they found the breakthrough was a complete failure.

The sun is trying to break through the clouds. A glare of silvery platinum casts a bright shadow between the snow-brushed hills of Belgium. All is quiet and serene. Clouds are moving at a fast pace. Fresh flurries occasionally coat the old to hide all indications of movement or trespassing. Snow is good camouflage.

The village folks mourn and bury the dead. An old man told me he lost four children during the barrage from artillery. They suffer tragedy and hold no resentment toward us. Civilians in small villages suffer most. Damn this war. The longer it continues, the less we understand the causes we are fighting for.

January 19, 1945

If this so-called rest period hasn't been of any good, at least it has given me a chance to clean up. I went to Barvaux today for a shower and a clean change of clothing. I can't see how anyone can rest merely by sleeping in dugouts and hugging fires during the day. The temperature took a sharp drop today. Freezing weather and wind prevailed. We haven't been doing anything these past few days. One consolation is the extreme quiet. Snow is falling, adding several inches to what had already piled up.

The mountaintops of the Ardennes in Belgium are high and steep. Fir trees can be seen for miles around up and down the valleys. The scenery is beautiful. Any indication of battles having taken place among these hills during the past few weeks is now covered in deep snow. The pure whiteness of the snow throws a heavenly serenity on the slopes leading down to the valleys. Snow can make the present seem so normal once again.

Men have fought and died in these hills. We shelled the hell out of this very position before taking over, and now, as I look about, even the village in all its darkness and sorrow seems to glisten with the purity of the fresh air and the arrival of the snow.

The night is cold and miserable. My thoughts wander back in time. I think of the battery of the past and the battery of the present. To me, most of the boys seem to have aged much. Smiles are few. The senselessness of the war is written very plainly upon the faces of Dix, Lineham, Thomashefsky, and many others. I suppose we all have aged somewhat. War is a horrific strain on a man physically and mentally. We cuss, swear, and talk very uncleanly. Our thoughts are constantly of home. We are here in body only. We ask when this damned war will end. When will we go home? Will we ever get furloughs? Which sector of the front lines will we go to now? And then the massacre of Malmedy happens to arouse our anger—a hundred men killed in mass murder.

January 20, 1945

We are on the front lines once again. Our rest prevailed only five days. We advanced fifteen miles today, passing many wrecked American Sherman tanks. It seems as though our tanks come out second best in this sector. We are deep in the Bulge. A barn is our sleeping quarters for the night.

2100
January 22, 1945

We just finished a late supper. My section just returned from our former position and had a heck of a time. Every one of us is sick and tired. We are now way up in the front lines, very close to the doughboys. This new position it is hot with mortar fire. We had a close call with our entire section. Airbursts are all around us. I can't stomach the sight of the dead. I don't like to look at them. We came back in the dark on the return trip. I believe it is much safer to travel at night. With the passing of each day, conditions become much rougher. Let's have an end to this damn mess. We are aging quickly.

0500
January 23, 1945

Just came off guard. The morning is clear and dry. Mortars are firing quite often. Lieutenant Chrisman said he had hoped we wouldn't make the return trip in the dark. It seems as though some of the boys had their fingers crossed for us. However, this is hard to conceive of, because no one seems too concerned for the dead.

We have had perfect targets in the clear openings on both occasions of our return to our new position.

Sophie, many times you have come close to being a widow. Let's not make it too close.

January 23, 1945

As we came to this position late yesterday afternoon, the German front lines were only about three miles away, and now, thirty-six hours later, they have withdrawn to about twelve hundred yards. I slept in the hayloft of a barn last night.

We prepared for march order today. Rumors are that we are going to the rear, possibly to Liège for a week's rest. This sector is rather quiet now. We are still in position to fire. Only in several instances did the liaison officer call for any artillery fire from our sector.

We have a nice setup tonight—that is to say, nice compared to what we have had these past several weeks. Werbicki, Dick, Bill, Mock, Campbell, Landry, and I occupy the front room of a home. We have a stove. We are a little crowded; however, we are warm.

Since arriving in the European theater of operations, I've slept in German basements, pillboxes, dugouts, attics, barns, and haylofts. Many of these quarters were formerly occupied by Germans. We know because they leave much of their equipment behind as evidence.

The name of this village is Bovigny. It has been shattered by artillery fire, however not as much as the others that we have been through.

Our guns are situated beyond the village in about sixteen inches of snow. The countryside in this vicinity is slopy, but we can readily see we are nearing the foot of the Ardennes mountain chain and approaching the plains of the nearing Rhineland. We now stand only a few miles from the fifth. The Eighty-Fourth Division played the center throughout the entire engagement of the Battle of the Bulge, and now, with the closing of the gap, we are being flanked by the north and south forces, resulting in our forces being left in the rear. Our mission has been accomplished in this sector. We participated for thirty-seven days in this battle and have seen much destruction. We endured bitterly cold weather and handled much ammunition. War is disgustingly hard work. War is brutal and inhumane. War is hell.

Part III

2000

February 1, 1945

May this book be a continuation of my last writings. With the will of God, I sincerely wish that to read the contents of my previous writings and the writings of this book to my dear wife within the near future.

Sergeant Frank Pappas

Awans, Belgium

February 1, 1945

During the past five days, we have been resting in a cellar, catching up on much-needed rest. There isn't much to write of. The people of this community have welcomed us into their homes. The one consolation is the realization that this village has been spared the destruction of warfare. Landry, Bill, Joe, and I have taken refuge with an elderly couple who have treated us very warmly. They look upon us as four sons and try every means of providing the comforts of home. When we left Bovigny, our last battle position, only five days ago, the snow was still knee-deep. Now, with three days of almost continuous rainfall, much of the snow has disappeared.

We have lived a quiet and peaceful life since coming away from the battlefront. The nights are quiet with no artillery or mortar fire to contend with. The excitement and strain of warfare is lacking, and if this rest continues, any addition to my writing will be rather dull and monotonous—a very far cry from my days at Geilenkirchen and the Bulge.

We are moving up to the front lines once again this Saturday, and this I hate very much. We have been living a lazy man's life for the past several days, and now they intend to bring us in once again for the final blow.

Germany

February 3, 1945

At six thirty last night, we said good-bye to Mom and Pop and started back on our long journey to Germany. At one thirty in the morning, we entered the ghost town of Aachen, our first indication that we were once again within the border of Germany. Aachen is a fairly large city. With the aid of a clear night and a fairly bright moon up, I did have a good glimpse of the town's wreckage. It must have been a beautiful and prosperous city at one time. Many German cities are.

We are now in a small German town only five miles from Neuenkirchen, precisely the same sector we left forty-eight days ago to follow up on the Battle of the Bulge. We made this return trip with the strictest of secrecy, moving out of Belgium in a blackout with all identifications and insignias removed. We are now under strict censorship. We will strike once again. Where or when, we do not know. However, we do know the Rhine is our objective, and all indications point to a terrific battle.

Unknown, Germany
February 4, 1945

Although since entering Germany we have been several miles away from German artillery fire, we still must contend with Jerry planes. He has been flying over the town for the past hour, dropping antipersonnel bombs. Washing Machine Charlie is constantly looking for trouble. He usually drops flares and then follows up by dropping his load. A few were dropped in the distance only a few seconds ago, and it shook the building slightly.

Once again, we slush in stinking, dirty mud. When we move into position, I'm afraid we shall mire down. I can hear many bombs bursting somewhere in the not-too-far distance. Here comes Charlie to pay us another visit.

I don't know the name of this town; however, it isn't badly damaged. The house that my section is occupying is slightly damaged. We have not done much since coming here. We are standing by, waiting for orders to shove off. When those will come, we don't know, but in the meantime, we are taking it easy. Werbicki has a little trouble in writing his letters, where as Mock seems to concentrate very much so. The general attitude and disposition of the boys gives one the impression that we are thousands of miles away from the front lines.

Lindern, Germany
February 6, 1945

Once again we are on the front lines. We came into position last night in a complete blackout. We did have some assistance from the British searchlights; however, that was short-lived, as we soon approached to the front lines.

Weeks ago, we shelled the hell out of Lindern, giving our infantry the support to capture the town. Lindern is badly damaged. We are now only about a mile or so from the Ruhr river. The elements of earth and sky have treated us rather fairly in this position. The ground is hard, and the rain has done little to hinder maneuvering.

No matter how tough conditions become, men always have time to laugh and joke. Stories and slurs fly thick and fast.

Mock is a great storyteller. Dick and Werbicki can't be beat in slurring.

Germany is slowly but surely being destroyed. Every square mile of land taken by our armies thus far has been overrun and destroyed. Towns and villages are barely recognizable by name. Homes and business establishments are destroyed by artillery, and if they survive this attack, then we destroy them once the infantry enters the town and takes over. This really is a crime. We chop up doors, furniture, and whatnot to make fires. The Germans shall hate us for our doings. This home we are staying in now has been damaged very badly; however, the ground floor protects us from the weather. It offers better protection against shrapnel. Luckily it is uncomfortably quiet around here.

Lindern, Germany
February 7, 1945

Today we moved into a house that offers much better protection. We are in the cellar of a home. The structure of this ground floor is similar to what we had at Geilenkirchen. It is amazing the way these cellars remain undamaged by artillery fire. The upper structure of this building is entirely destroyed, and the cellar remains undamaged. I believe we have good protection here.

Since coming into position, we have been preparing for this drive. We have much ammunition at the position, and no doubt we will receive more. Every move will be coordinated. I sincerely hope this will be the last and final push. May the gods of war grant us final victory, and may the angels of mercy be kind to us.

Sophie, this may decide if our prayers and wishes will be answered. Keep your fingers crossed, dear. The end seems to be so near, and yet nearing the end, I am afraid to say this may be our toughest battle.

All the boys seem to be comfortable and at ease once again. Cellars make one seem so much more comfortable, although many times in the past, we slept and lived in the open under artillery and mortar fire. Mock is writing a letter, Dick is eating a K ration, and Landry is relaxing. Bill and Campbell are talking. And to think this is war, and we are on the front lines. We are relaxing now, but in a few more hours, we shall sweat and cuss and wish to hell that we had never taken part in this drive.

Hell may be far from pleasant, but I'm sure it can't be any worse than war. War is hell.

Lindern, Germany
February 8, 1945

Thoughts and feelings have a tendency to become radical. We ask why there must be a final battle to bring this war to an end. Why must men die so near the end? Why must we satisfy the thriving anxiety of future historians by bringing this war to a spectacular and colorful end? Why can't this war come to a quiet end this very moment and spare the lives of those who inevitably will die in this final drive for the vitals of Germany? Historians will build and write a wonderful story about this push. But why? Many lives will be sacrificed to make this story possible.

The night is quiet. Many British searchlights are lighting up the skies. Jerry lobbed a few shells in our area this afternoon.

In a few hours, the drive will commence. We are prepared for the final blow. We anticipate heavy resistance. The elements of Mother Nature are our biggest enemy in this drive. We must cross the Ruhr River. If plans go according to schedule, we will be the second artillery battalion to cross the Ruhr River. The Germans have the advantage of well-dug-in fortifications between the Ruhr River and the Rhine River. The distance between both rivers is only twenty miles, so we can expect much artillery fire from the enemy east of the Rhine. If they move the weapons, we know we shall be in for a hot battle, because they have had the time to prepare for a defensive push. May the historians live in all their glory of enthusiasm, because we do not anticipate halting until we cross the Rhine, our major objective.

Lindern, Germany
February 9, 1945

Another day has come and gone, and here we are, still waiting for the go-ahead signal to open up. Many of us are not too eager to face this big offensive because we clearly understand what to expect. We have been informed as to how we should participate in this drive. We shall spearhead through in crossing the Ruhr River, and with our right flank left wide-open, we can very well expect much counterfire from that direction. We may encounter Germans during our advance because the infantry will not halt to mop up.

General Monty Montgomery, our commanding officer, has put out a message of the day, stating, "Regardless of all cost and sacrifices, we must and shall make this drive a complete success."

The following is a message to my wife.

Dearest Sophie,

There is a time in a man's life when he thinks. He remembers the past. He hopes for the future. He wonders what the outcome of the next few days shall mean to him and how they will affect his loved ones. Sophie, the climax is very close. Throughout this, the memory of you has been constantly with me. Once again, we will face the enemy, possibly for the last time. So far I have been lucky. Can it be that your prayers and wishes have been heard? I hope so, for so much depends on the next few days. The end is much too near for me to die now.

Always remember, dear, it is only you whom I've loved so dearly, and it shall be only you who will hear my call.

Yours forever, Frank

Werbicki, Mock, and I are still up. Since arriving in Lindern, we have been keeping late hours. The one advantage we have in Germany is that we can almost always find a cellar and set up house somewhat comfortably. This anticipated drive may boomerang. The Jerries have blown up the dams backing up the Ruhr River, which undoubtedly will hinder if not halt the coming drive.

The sun made an appearance today after an absence of three days. Lindern is thriving in water and mud. Very little remains of this once quaint town. Our artillery plays havoc and destruction on all German cities and towns. We are situated by the railroad tracks that lead to Geilenkirchen.

Farina is back with us. He was wounded in the early days of our participation of this war. He spent two months in England recovering from his wounds. He is the only one of all those wounded in our battery to return. To me, he doesn't appear to be fully recovered. The morale of the fifth section was very high this evening. You just can't keep these boys down. There's never a dull moment for us. We have been in rough spots and hot spots, and the spirit and morale never change.

The night is cold, wet, dark, and very dreary. It has been drizzling continuously all day. Jerry shells have been coming in frequently today. Six Jerry planes flew over our position today. We have plenty of firepower around here. This continuous rain isn't helping us any. Our drive has been postponed indefinitely. The Ruhr River has overrun, and the rainfall isn't helping us either.

We'll open up one of these days, and when we do, there will be hell to pay. The Germans are a stubborn lot, and it is certain they will put up a stiff resistance. This will be our third campaign since coming to the front lines. We are now entitled to two stars: the Battle of the Rhine and the Battle of the Bulge.

Everything is mostly quiet tonight. An occasional shell burst is the only indication of any enemy resistance. Someday soon the fireworks will start, and when they do, look out.

We left Belgium like a house on fire with the strictest of secrecy. We came into position at Lindern in complete darkness. We were warned of revealing any military information time and time again, and what happened? We stayed in position five days, giving Jerry all the time in the world to spot us. Today, they sent in several barrages that were too darn close for comfort. They have spotted us, so we can now expect artillery fire. Damn those shells. They certainly come in fast. We can hear the muzzle blast, and in a few seconds—*boom!* Our drive is now halted. The Ruhr River is rising. The Germans try every means of ways to halt our advance. An occasional enemy shell coming in is a good lesson to awaken us to the fact that we are on the front lines. When things are quiet for several days, most everyone becomes rather lax and stays out in the open too much. Today's barrages put everyone undercover again.

Dick blew his top this evening. He asked, "Why must we live like this? Why must we be blown to bits? Do they think we are animals?" My only answer to his question was this. If Dick, Bill, Joe, and the likes of these boys west of the Ruhr and Fritz, Hans, Otto, and the likes of those boys east of the Ruhr awaken to the fact that they are the tools and victims of the few in power and unite, the results may be entirely different. The fact is we are both fighting for a cause that probably never existed. Nevertheless, we are led to believe, we are led to hate, we are led to mistrust, and we are led to die and fight against each other's beliefs. We are the victims of propaganda, diplomacy, and interloping treachery.

Lindern, Germany
February 14, 1945

Just as I had expected, Jerry sent in everything today—artillery fire from rows of guns to robot bombs. Luckily we suffered no casualties. One of our tractors was damaged by shrapnel and set on fire. It isn't safe to wander around. The artillery barrages sent by the Germans to date don't compare with Geilenkirchen.

Our fire consists mostly of harassing fire. The front lines are swamped in mud. We haven't the slightest idea what we are going to do now. The Ruhr River is flooded, we can't advance any closer, and the longer we stay here, the more certain we are that Jerry is really going to zero in someday and run us out.

Lindern, Germany
0230
February 17, 1945

I feel pretty darn sleepy. The time is two thirty in the morning, and everything is quiet on the Western Front. We haven't had much action during the last three days. A few robot bombs came over very low the other morning. An occasional burp gun or machine gun may be heard. An occasional enemy artillery barrage hits us as well. Aside from that, the Ninth Army's lines are at a complete standstill.

We have now been in this position eleven days. I never thought we would be here this long. I am glad we gave the cellar a good cleanup the day we moved in. This is the best setup we've had since coming to the European theater of operations.

I can't remember any finer weather since our arrival overseas. Spring is in the air. I'm too sleepy to continue.

The time is one forty-five on Sunday morning. German artillery opened up a stiff barrage at one thirty that had the properties of a jump-off drive. The barrage only lasted about twenty-five minutes, but they certainly threw in many shells in those few minutes. Many of them whistled directly over our heads. A good many landed in the Ruhr River. The barrage was big enough to cause many casualties. It seems as though the Jerries have dared us to come out and fight. Jerry knows we are up here on the line. They threw leaflets onto our highways welcoming the Eighty-Fourth Division back to Germany. Jerry still has plenty of guts left, and he is now fully prepared to meet our drive. Considering the barrage they threw in a few minutes ago, I believe we are in for a stiff battle.

Mock, Werbicki, and I are still up. I have been writing letters for the past few hours. I recall writing letters under many different circumstances, during artillery barrages both pro and counter, during snowstorms, during heavy rainfall, during air attacks, and during counterattacks from the enemy.

We have been experiencing beautiful weather. Artillery fire, both the enemy's and ours, has been frequently heavy. We can hear machine-gun fire in the not-too-far distance.

Mock is still writing his letter. Werbicki is just about ready to close off. How long will we continue to keep these late hours? This is the best setup we've had as far as gun positions are concerned, so we are taking advantage of it. Werbicki's tractor furnishes the lights, and we have a good stove and good mattresses to sleep on. Yes, this is the front lines, and we are combat soldiers. The amazing thing about combat soldiers is that they are so nonchalant and unaware of the predicament they are in and the circumstances that may follow.

For the past ten minutes, a large formation of American bombers has been flying over our sector toward the vitals of Germany. The droning of the motors is endless. Jerry is going to take a pasting tonight. Someone is flying very low over our position.

Corporal Norris and Meisel were badly burned this evening in their dugout when someone carelessly tossed a cigarette butt into a powder charge. Both boys received second degree burns about the face and hands. Someday a few of these boys should awaken to the fact that powder charges are dangerous and shouldn't be laid or tossed around so carelessly.

Lindern, Germany
0100
February 23, 1945

The day for the big push has arrived. The Ruhr River has abated to almost normal. One hour and a half from now, the Western Front will be ablaze with our artillery fire. This will be the knockout blow, regardless of the cost. Plans have been changed from what was originally decided. If everything goes well, we will cross the Ruhr River on D plus 3. Forty-five minutes after we open our barrages, our infantry will make the first major assault on the east banks without tank support. They will depend solely upon our artillery. This will be a slaughter.

For the past fourteen days, we have been taking it easy. Now we will put out as much as we can, because this will mean the end of the war if we are successful.

Many of us will not live to see the end. At the moment, I have no fear. The morale in general is high. Landry is doing a darn good imitation of Donald Duck. Campbell is full of jokes and wisecracks. Dick is unusually quiet. He usually is whenever tense moments arrive.

The time is getting closer. Enough ammo is at the guns for the initial barrages. May God be with those infantry boys, they are in for a tough time.

If this drive is the final success leading toward victory, it will only be because of the sacrifice of many lives.

God bless us all. Sophie, I'll be thinking of you throughout. Dearest, I am not afraid; however, I am deeply concerned because we have waited so long for a happy and permanent reunion, and now it is this final battle that will decide if our prayers will be answered. God have mercy on us.

Linder, Germany
0300
February 23, 1945

This is it. For the past fifteen minutes, every piece of artillery we have on this front has opened up and fired continuously.

The noise is terrific, and no doubt the attacks are very devastating. Each volley of each battery, battalion, and division sends out a thundering roar that shakes the earth. Will the Germans take it? Our doughboys must be sweating it out. They will attempt to cross the Ruhr River in another twenty minutes. I am glad that we are not on the receiving end. The artillery is terrific.

The Ruhr River has been crossed by our doughboys. At three thirty this morning, they jumped off, and within a half hour, Korrenzig was taken without much opposition. We fired for nine and a half hours without letup. I had a ringside seat this afternoon, watching our bombers unloose over the German lines. Enemy ack-ack artillery was light. We spent most of the day at the gun positions. Although our barrages were terrific, Jerry still has the will to toss in a few impacts on the high buttes. We may cross the Ruhr River tomorrow. The weather has been fine throughout. Infantry boys have been passing our position all evening, going up to the front lines.

The Eighty-Fourth once again comes out on top. May we continue with the very least of sacrifices and make this attack a total and complete victory.

Lindern, Germany
1100
February 26, 1945

We are standing by to advance forward within the next few hours. Our artillery has been firing almost continuously ever since the drive initially began. Thousands upon thousands of rounds have been fired across the Ruhr River.

Enemy planes have been flying over our positions. Our ack-ack was terrific. Jerry planes blew out our bridge across the Ruhr River.

German resistance is rather stiff. We are not advancing as swiftly as we anticipated. Our battalion accounted for knocking out three enemy gun batteries yesterday. Enemy artillery fire is still coming in close. This is the third day of the battle, and all probability points to a long, drawn-out battle.

Lindern, Germany
1400
February 26, 1945

We may not pull out today. The Germans have been counterattacking. The forward observer says the position we are to move into is still being shelled.

The morale of the ammunition section is rather high. As an example of the humor being tossed about, Dick said, "The fire went out." Campbell replied, "How can it? The doors are closed." Remarks such as those go on continuously.

German bombers have been unloading close to our position. Although we are on the offensive, things get pretty hot around here too. The doughboys are the ones who really have it tough. Sherman tanks have been going forward all morning.

We arrived under the protection of darkness into this burg last night. We traveled ahead of the infantry with our left flank exposed to the enemy. The artillery at times gets too close to the enemy. However, we have had the Germans on the run ever since we crossed the Ruhr River three days ago at the break of dawn. We have worked hard to make this drive a success. Much ammunition has been fired. Our artillery is devastating. I've seen Jerries blown to bits. It's a sickening sight. We are traveling so fast that there is little time for the medics to bury the dead. The only fortifications we are encountering are trenches, and brother, the Germans are throwing up their arms.

What a war. Frank is playing Red-Hot Boogie on the piano. We are staying in a wonderful home. I am now writing at the desk in a library of a once wonderful house. This burg hasn't been shelled, so the homes are in very good condition. However, we have ransacked the hell out of them.

The ammunition is breaking my section's back. We really put out the ammo for this drive.

After crossing the Ruhr River, we arrived in Baal. Very little was left of Baal. It is a complete wreck. We are moving swiftly. We have march orders to advance once again. It seems as though we are only making one-night stands at each town we reach—a far cry from the days when we stayed in a position for a week or two and fired continuously. If the prisoners keep coming in as they have, we should reach the Rhine River very soon. Our infantry has been doing darn good work. We arrived in this burg so quickly last night that the Krauts left warm meals on the table. Today is the first chance I've had to write since the night before we crossed the Ruhr River. Our engineers certainly did build a good bridge.

The east and west banks of the Ruhr River were mauled inch by inch. I can't imagine how anyone survived our initial barrages on the opening days of the drive.

The Jerry civilians are a sorry sight. May this war teach them that militarism does not pay. They have suffered and now know the devastation and tragedy of warfare. May they open their eyes and see for a change. If it wasn't for their antagonism, many of us would not be here today. Damn the Germans. May they learn in defeat and make amends in the coming peace.

Village Bain, Germany
March 1, 1945

We marched as ordered this afternoon, advancing to our new position. Our advance was so rapid we never did give the German civilians a chance to go deeper into the fatherland. We are right up with the doughboys. We passed several platoons who were dug in. A few had .30-caliber machine guns mounted right by their foxholes. We were at the time only several hundred yards from the enemy. On the way up here, the entire highway was strewn with wreckage, supplies, and dead horses. We saw many more prisoners this morning and this afternoon.

There are at least one hundred civilians in this barn under our custody. C Battery is standing guard over them. A few did belong to the Volkssturm; the older people are a pitiful sight. A near panic was started this afternoon when our guns fired. People at home should be thankful that they are not going through this ordeal. It's wicked.

Unknown, Germany
March 3, 1945

The time is 0300. This barnstorming across the Rhine is getting tiresome. I have had very little sleep in the last five days. Roughly, we have traveled at least thirty-five miles in this drive so far. We expect to reach the Rhine River sometime in the morning.

Enemy resistance has been light. They are withdrawing in an orderly fashion. We haven't seen too many dead Jerries during this drive. What few I did see certainly were plastered.

We haven't yet stayed in any position more than a day. Loading and unloading seems to have become second nature. We billeted in a house last night once occupied by German officers. We tried the uniforms on—a perfect fit.

I will try to get a little shut-eye now. We will be going forward in the morning.

On the Rhine in Germany
2400
March 7, 1945

We drove clear across the Rhineland. We reached our line or sector of firing in complete blackout last night. We can now stand on a high point and see the Rhine River. We may be here for quite some time. Jerry still seems to be very persistent. We drove and have worked hard for the past ten days. We've had very little play. Two hours after coming into position, we were firing across the Rhine River at designated targets. It seems to me that this is going to be a repetition of the Ruhr River. I had a close call yesterday while unloading ammo. As I unloaded the first piece, a shell burst only fifty yards away. Our trucks protected us from shrapnel. Jerry has been tossing them in today—a fairly good sign that they have a line of offensive once again. Now we must cross the Rhine River, but when? That is the question.

On the Rhine in Germany
0215
March 8, 1945

We had a chief-of-section meeting this afternoon, and I was told we may be on the banks of the Rhine River for quite some time. Activity has been very quiet. We are taking it easy once again. When war comes to a standstill, there isn't too much to do, especially when a body of water separates us from the enemy. We did anticipate an early crossing of the Rhine, but Jerry beat us to the punch by blowing out the east end of the bridge.

This is a darn good gun position. Dick, Joe, and I set up quarters in the basement of a home, and we have a comfortable little setup.

On the Rhine in Germany
0100
March 9, 1945

We have been shelling Duisburg and its surroundings for the past two days. It is more or less a softening-up process. We have plenty of ammo on hand. Occasionally, this sector becomes very quiet. I see where the First and Third Armies are going to town. As usual, they get full credit.

The weather is fine. This is the best gun position we have ever been in. The quarters are fine as well; we now have electricity furnished by a German power plant. The one advantage of this swift drive is that there was no time for the Germans to destroy the water and electrical power plants. Many of the Germans try to be friendly, but regardless, we still intend to cross the Rhine River. The east bank of the Rhine River is now ablaze from our artillery.

Rhine in Germany
March 12, 1945

We don't know what the score is. We were told we may stay in this position for at least two weeks. Why don't we just cross the Rhine River? Why give the First and Third Armies all the credit? We fought as hard as they did. In fact, we met stiffer resistance throughout. To top it off, we advanced and covered many more miles.

We haven't been doing much during the past few days. Thus far, we have had very little counterbattery attack. Sometimes it's so quiet around here it's hard to conceive that a war is going on. Bond came back to the battery yesterday. He was hurt on our way to Belgium during the German breakthrough. Everyone is in good spirits. Nothing exciting or unusual has happened during the past week.

While the drive to the Rhine River lasted, it was exciting and fast. However, the situation has come to a standstill. By the way, we moved to a newer position. As usual, if we have a good setup, it invariably doesn't last long. However, this setup has no water and no electricity. We have lived under worse conditions in the past. My, how time flies. It seems like it was only yesterday we were shivering in the hills of Belgium.

Lieutenant Turpin appears to be a likeable sort of a guy. I had quite a discussion with him today. Lieutenant Ramsing is okay, but I wish to hell he wouldn't worry too much about the damn ammunition.

No doubt Jerry doesn't know we are here. Not a round has landed in our position yet, and we have been here five days.

Are we fighting to win the war, or are we fighting to see how close to schedule we can stay? Why didn't we cross the Rhine instead of coming to a standstill? When we first reached the Rhine, we should never have halted. No doubt Jerry had defenses set up east of the Rhine that we could have made a beachhead of without too much opposition. We had the ammo—loads and loads of it. Our artillery could have pulverized the east bank of the Rhine.

The situation is different now. Jerry has had plenty of time to dig in. Here we sit now, doing nothing. We haven't fired much. A battalion of 4.5 situated to our direct rear opened up with a steady barrage early this evening, which lasted at least a half an hour. I wonder what they spotted. It was pretty hot while it lasted.

I wonder what impression the German civilians had of us today, seeing us playing football and baseball practically under the very eyes of the German army. We Americans are certainly a cocky bunch. Poker games, craps games, and radio tinkering are the main issues for this 327th Field Artillery Battalion on the front lines today.

I went to the rear today, back to Krefeld, to hear the general make a speech. It was the usual baloney about how well we fought and how proud he was of the Eighty-Fourth.

Krefeld was more interesting than the speech. This large town certainly took an American shellacking from air attacks. Pretty darn good, I say. Front line troops are taking calisthenics. We haven't had enough to do for the past four and a half months. I'm thankful to be alive, let alone to take calisthenics. Oh, hell, this can't go on forever. Until then, I'm going to bed.

Every time our artillery opens up, half the ceiling comes toppling down. Not much of the plaster is left. Each volley makes this house shake and quiver like Jello. A forward observer must have spotted something worth shooting at.

Since reaching the Rhine, we have been at a complete standstill. There isn't much to be done. We have been taking it rather easy. This is a pleasant position. No indications whatsoever can be seen of war destruction. Days are getting longer—a good sign of spring.

Today is the first day of spring, a most beautiful and wonderful sunny day. Shrubs and trees are showing their plentiful buds. An added richness has been blended into the newly grown grass along the banks. We are all comfortably warm and dry. Everyone is in high spirits. Spring is so enlivening that one momentarily forgets the war and dreams of the past.

The Ninth Army front is quiet—extremely quiet. Something is in the air. We are setting up dummy gun positions to deceive the German observers. We have orders to make these positions so realistic that even the civilians still living in the vicinity are fooled.

Rumors are several divisions are pulling out to cross the Rhine in the British sector to drive a path for us to make another spearhead. The general staff appears to be very pleased with our successful spearhead drive across the Rhineland a couple of weeks ago.

Most of the activity now is down in the First and Third Army sectors. We will open up again in the future. The Ninth Army may yet decide to final victory in this war, with the Eighty-Fourth Division spearheading the advance.

We went on a search today and came across a former German position of 88s. There were at least eight there; however, we only took two. The Jerries abandoned them during the quick withdrawal. We will use them in our dummy positions. If headquarters wants realism, what could be any better than 88s? An 88 is a wonderful gun. The mechanism is so easy to elevate or traverse, and the tube is menacingly long and frightening. Those are the babies that gave us so much trouble at Geilenkirchen. How many times did I hit the ground? Jerry certainly left many 88s behind in his hasty run to the Rhine.

We will have our dummy positions completed in a couple of days. Activity is very light.

Almost three weeks of inactivity were suddenly broken at three o'clock this morning. The crossing of the Rhine is on. The entire Ninth Army front opened up a stiff preparation lasting four hours. The thundering roar was terrific, coming from guns of all calibers. Darkness was broken into an endless flash along the entire riverbank. Fires can be seen along the entire east bank. Our artillery was devastating. C Battery alone fired 340 rounds in less than four hours.

This attack was a complete surprise to all of us. Six hours before the initial barrage, we were informed of the coming attack and just how we would participate. Little news is coming out as to the results of the crossing. This was an artillery battle on a large scale, with seventy-eight artillery battalions participating.

On the Rhine
2300
March 24, 1945

After the terrific pounding we gave the Jerries early this morning, the Luftwaffe is now flying overhead, looking for trouble. They have been over our position for the past couple of hours, strafing and dropping bombs.

The latest reports say bridgeheads have been made across the Rhine and progress is being made.

The day in itself was very warm.

Jerry shells are now coming in darn close. High bursts are all around us.

On the Rhine
2245
March 25, 1945

Palm Sunday will soon be something of the past.

Jerry planes have been flying over our position all evening. Our artillery has been shelling the east bank of the Rhine since early this evening. A few Jerry shells also came in. Jerry does most of his firing at night. The rippling, roaring thunder of artillery can be heard clear across the Rhine River.

This war hasn't halted our ball games. Much sport playing goes on despite the war. Shows go on, and showers are available daily. This is a modern war. In this position, I've managed to stay very clean. We may jump off soon, and if we do, it is only then that we will become grimy and dirty once again.

On the Rhine
March 29, 1945

Early this morning, Jerry sent in a few very close rounds. Aside from that activity, it has been very quiet on this side of the Rhine.

We of the Eighty-Fourth have been held back as the ace in the hole for this drive across the Rhine. We are crossing in a couple of days, and once we start rolling, we aren't going to stop.

We have rested well and are in tip-top shape. Guns and vehicles are in the best of condition.

Peace and serene quiet have fallen upon the Rhineland once again. The civilians are going about their spring plowing. The grass is really green. The Rhineland is beautiful. There are no signs of neglect or wild weeds. The people through the years of preservation have cared for the Rhineland soil.

Germany never lacked the beauty that nature so willingly bestows upon mother earth. Germany is beauty in every sense of the human type. Green valleys, rolling hills, running streams, superhighways, land on either side with tall trees, small cottages, and wonderful homes and chateaus give Germany a beauty of simplicity so rare and fine.

East of the Rhine
April 2, 1945

We finally moved across the Rhine River after occupying and holding down position on the west bank of the Rhine for three weeks. We journeyed north, crossing the Rhine at Wessel. Based on the destruction done, it seems as though a tough battle was fought on both sides of the Rhine in this particular sector. I noticed two bridges that had been completely destroyed. The river is only about two hundred yards wide; however, it is a swiftly running river.

After traveling east about six miles, we came to the sector where the airborne division had landed a week or so ago. Gliders and trailers were numerous. It appeared to be at least a thousand if not possibly much more left on the open fields. Many were damaged, but not to a very great extent. The countryside throughout the entire trip was beautiful. We passed a couple of fairly large towns that had been totally destroyed. We traveled a distance of fifty-two miles and are now in a wooded pine area, offering a very clear reminiscence of the Louisiana maneuvers. The scenery seems so familiar. It is hard to conceive that we are in Germany and not Louisiana.

This is a staging area far to the rear of the lines. We will move out tonight and possibly go into position at our next destination. Possibly once again we will meet the enemy and stage a running battle. Let's wish we all reach Berlin in a very short time. Best of luck to all of us.

Across the Rhine
April 3, 1945

We are still in the wooded pine area. Early yesterday afternoon, we were told we would march-order in blackout, and then we changed and bedded down for the night. I slept in the tractor, and so did Joe, Bill, and Chet. Darn good thing that we did, for it poured like the dickens early in the morning. It is midafternoon now, and we are lined up in the wooded area, waiting for march orders. The scenery, the fires, and the usual huddle of men take me back to Louisiana. This is the first and only position we've ever occupied that reminded us in the least of the States.

Since crossing the Rhine, we have traveled 135 miles east. The scenery of Germany is most captivating and amazing in its beauty. If the term *fatherland* means "a little bit of heaven," then Germany is it, for it is in every sense of the word beautiful. Rolling hills, beautiful forests, sparkling streams, and richly cultivated farmhouses make up Germany's wonderful scenery.

We have traveled fast at a steady pace. Passing Munster, one can see that she was a beautiful and scenic city at one time. A man can crash a beautiful vase into a thousand pieces, but as it lies there on the floor, he knows it once was a creation of wonderful art. The same holds true for most of the German cities.

Thus far, we hadn't encountered enemy resistance—until today, when we reached the Weser River. We are now in the Weser Valley, beautiful and naturally scenic. The hills are high, the scattered rooftops glowing red, creating a beautiful contrast with the green countryside. Our guns are on a hillside pointing in east toward a high hilltop overlooking the peaceful valley. Peace in this wonderful and beautiful country would be heavenly. These people are fools to ever want to war against the world.

We are heading for Berlin. During our dash across the Rhine, we passed thousands upon thousands of refugees of all nationalities, their possessions predominating. Wreckages are very few; the Germans haven't offered any resistance.

On the first night after our crossing, we slept in the wooded pine area, the second night in a barn, and the third night in another barn, and tonight, we share a civilian's home. We are in reserve and so have enjoyed the long and scenic ride. Today is actually the first time we have gone into position.

My impression of the refugees now is decidedly different from what I had previously thought. They appear to have been well fed, although there is a blank or just lost expression upon their faces. I am not so sure that they are truthfully glad to have been freed. Their anxiety can be a false truth within themselves.

Being in reserve suits us all well enough. We have had our share of battles and are now hoping to go along only for the ride.

May it be so. Amen!

April 8, 1945

The sunset this evening was an artist's dream come true. Looking from the bay window across the green stretch, I watched as the sunset threw its warm colors upon the glistening lake. In the not-too-far distance, the hills were making a stretch for the sun, slowly pulling it below the horizon. It's a beautiful day in April, and yet we are reminded a war is still in progress, for only a few minutes ago, four Messerschmitts flew over our positions. Our ack-ack opened a continuous fire upon them, tracers leaving a distinct path in the blue sky. Many Messerschmitts flew around several times, those pesky dogs.

We are only seven miles from Hanover. We have been moving continuously since our Rhine crossing to catch up with the enemy. We encountered enemy soldiers several times, but they never put up a stiff resistance.

Today we are in a new position. By the way, we crossed the Weser River yesterday. The scenery was incomparable. Racing across Germany, one easily forgets the war temporarily and observes the wondrous beauty of the countryside.

I slept in a most comfortable bed last night. We drank well and ate well. The homes are as comfortable and as clean as at home. Tonight, we enjoy the comforts of another comfortable home. The bed linens are made of goose feathers. Food and drinks are aplenty.

Many German prisoners are coming in. Across the field in the direction of fire, the forests are swamped with Jerry soldiers who are surrendering to us hourly.

Our race across Germany is done in one-night stands. We have enjoyed the comforts of several homes since the beginning of the drive. The German people were never deprived of the comforts of a wonderful home. Every home thus far through Germany lacks very little in ways to make living conditions enjoyable.

Our crossing of the Weser River was on a pontoon bridge. Along the mountainside, we noticed a well-camouflaged factory.

Going into position today, we passed a mine given up by the Germans only a couple of hours before our arrival. Several hundred slave workers delayed our route when they came out of the mines after the rescue. That was quite an experience, but most of us are looking for the end. We've had enough experience. Amen.

April 9, 1945

The time is 0400. Once again, we have moved forward. These one-night stands are taking us closer and closer to Berlin. Early yesterday morning, seventeen prisoners came out of the woods and gave themselves up to us in our last position.

We are now at a halt. Some Jerry armor has held us up. This afternoon, for the first time since coming to the European Theater of Operations, we used direct fire. At fifteen hundred yards, we fired upon the town, setting one building on fire and damaging several others. Jerry isn't leaving much equipment behind. For miles around, the land is untouched by warfare. At times it is hard to conceive that a war is in progress.

Tonight, I sleep on a sofa. Drinks are aplenty. Mostly everyone is drunk from wine twelve years old. Darn good stuff. We should all stay drunk for the duration.

Hanover
April 13, 1945

We have been in this position longer than we expected to be. This is a newer one since my last entry, a lovely and peaceful little community. Our artillery support has not been needed for the past several days. I occupy one of the cottages. If this were my home, I would now be at a beautiful and cozy little place. Our forward elements are traveling fast as hell.

We heard this morning that President Roosevelt died. He was not a man of destiny, because he never lived to finish his job.

Our long journey finally took us to Hanover. The Eighty-Fourth Division is credited for taking this city.

We didn't put an entry in for our last position, but it was a damn hot spot. Snipers and machine-gun fire were aplenty. German machine gunners were firing into our position, but they didn't last long. By morning everything was quiet.

We are not spearheading now, so we can expect every position from here on to be quiet and under control. This is our tenth position since crossing the Rhine. Our living quarters certainly have improved since the ugly days of Geilenkirchen. Instead of living in basements, we now take the top floors of houses with cozy, clean bedrooms and all the comforts of home. Luckily, we haven't encountered any artillery fire since our crossing of the Rhine. Jerry certainly has been withdrawing in a hurried and orderly fashion.

Unknown
April 16, 1945

We are deep in Germany, only eight miles from the Elbe River. The long journey across Germany has put a terrific wear and tear on our tractors. The old saying is "Berlin or bust." I have a hunch we are going to bust.

I don't know where we are now. After leaving the cottage, we made a sixty-mile push eastward and are now very much forward.

We are cut off by the enemy from our rear echelon. It looked bad for a while. I don't know what damage or casualties were incurred. The delay of mine is due to this situation we have encountered. The strength of the German breakthrough is supposedly five hundred men, twenty-two tanks, and five armored vehicles.

At the moment, our guns are pointing in the west, the direction we came from. We are not surrounded, but we are cut off from the rear. That was expected to happen sooner or later. We were going forward too fast.

The war goes on, and we still continue to live and eat well. We are set up in a small home with an electric washing machine, a couple of good stoves, and comfortable beds. What more can we ask for? And to think we are surrounded. The poor bastards don't know what they are getting themselves into when they surround us.

Unknown
April 17, 1945

We are now at the Elbe River. Artillery activity is pretty heavy from both sides. Finally, after a two-week dash across Ruhr, we ran into German artillery.

The Germans have still got us cut off from our rear. Supplies are having difficulty reaching us. I don't believe the situation is critical, because we did move forward yesterday to reach the Elbe. It's possible that a few little pockets need cleaning up.

We are living in a beautiful home. The furniture and glassware are beautiful and expensive. The home is of a modern design and has every means of comfort and desire. The grounds are made up of gardens and shrubbery. It is like a typical suburban home found in most American suburbs.

April 20, 1945

We are at a standstill now at the Elbe. German counterattacks have been frequent. Our left flank is threatened. We may move north to meet the counterattack. We are still cut off from our supplies. We have been firing often and are now running low on ammo. Well, we have been in target spots before, and I'm sure we have no need to be alarmed.

Unknown
April 22, 1945

For several days, we lived high, wide, and handsome, and suddenly we have march orders and we find ourselves in a farmhouse. It is quite a letdown from what we previously had. It was a messy-looking place, but it does look somewhat clean and orderly now.

Our move was so that we may consolidate our lines with the British. Plenty of firing goes on around here. Some German tanks are on the loose not too far away. Two Germans in the area forgot to duck. One of them was wounded elsewhere and staggered into the barn only a few feet away from our shack. He was pretty badly shot up. I see evidence of first aid being administered to him. The other Kraut is by the first gun. He was plastered coming out of a foxhole.

Throughout this entire drive, we came across very little German equipment. During this drive, we seemed to be more concerned with getting good living quarters and plenty to eat. Fresh eggs, freshly killed chickens, ham, and milk are our menu. The fifth section never goes hungry. Bill and Joe will find the food if there is any around. We live and eat well today, for tomorrow we may die. No truer words were ever spoken.

April 25, 1945

We as a battery have traveled a long and winding road during the last twenty-eight months. Tragedy and happiness played a big part in the making of the battery as a fighting unit. We are brothers and friends. We all have shared. We've eaten at the same table, piled in pup tents, shared packages from home, and talked of our personal affairs. In combat, we've worked and fought hard; seen buddies killed, and helped those who needed help. And now, after all these months, the men of the battery are fighting among themselves. We have whipped the Germans—are we trying to whip ourselves?

The Germans have left plenty of whiskey behind, and our boys are drinking it as though it were something heavenly. As I say, we have plenty to eat and drink. I put my good friend Dix to bed. We had quite a discussion tonight. Finally, I decided Dix had had about enough.

Chet entered and asked me why I don't associate with him as I did back in the States. He too had been drinking. Chet, to me, is the best friend any man could ever wish for.

Everything has been quiet for the past two days. We expect to link up with the Russians.

Bill, Dick, and I cleaned and cooked a couple of chickens today. I've been drinking a little tonight. I feel sleepy and tired. I have my wife's picture before me. It is early in the evening back home. I wonder what Sophie is doing on this day, April 25.

Unknown
April 26, 1945

The time is 0330. Everything is serenely and peacefully quiet in this war zone. Never since I arrived in the European theater of operations has it been so very quiet. A person is easily led to believe the war is over on a morning like this. The boys feel free once again. We haven't been in firing range for several days. The fifth section is feasting on fresh chicken and fresh milk. Every morning, the old lady gives us several gallons of fresh milk. Too bad we aren't staying here long. We all could regain some of the color and weight we have lost in battle. Even the boys are back on peaceful terms. The drinks have run out. I never did have trouble with any of my boys. In fact, most of the drunks come to me and tell me their troubles. The hour's getting late now. It's time for a little shut-eye.

Hindenburg
April 28, 1945

We as an artillery division have virtually seen the end of the war. In our six months of combat, we have shot up everything within our range, and now there is little left to shoot at. Our range is much too close to the Russians, and there is a possibility of cross fire. I haven't heard any artillery fire in over a week. We haven't done much of anything. We may do one of three things now: stay here as military troops, go home, or ship out for the China Burma India Theater. I would like to go home, but I'm afraid that this won't be so.

I met a Polish family this evening. They invited me over to spend another evening with them. We are now living in a home formerly owned by a major in the German army. It has already seen its best day; however, I imagine it once was a lovely home.

Hindenburg
April 30, 1945

I sit on a low, comfortably built chair, looking out the second-story window of this once magnificent home. I see across the courtyard a hill and gigantic tree only a few feet away. Branches make visibility from the window a little obscure. Barns and sheds outline the courtyard. The major must have been a gentleman farmer at one time.

The radio is close by, and it's playing Boogie-Woogie. I sit here and think of incidents that occurred during the past seven months. We thank God most of us are still together. For instance, if Joe has but one weakness, it is that he sleeps too much. I recall the open stretch of field we once crossed during an artillery barrage by the Germans. Joe was scared and said nothing better be in his way, because he was going to open up on the field. We raced across that field like a house on fire only to arrive in town and meet a concentration of fire. We were lucky. Joe will be a professional looter before this war is over.

And Bill—big, stout, good-hearted Bill—joined up with us in Belgium. Bill is from Jersey City and uses "them Brooklyn bums" lingo. He is a mighty handy fellow to have around. And Bauman, boyish and bright-eyed, is in his glory now with all the farmland we have overrun. He does his daily chores and even slaughtered a cow last evening when she couldn't give birth. It was the first time in my life that I saw a cow butchered. And of course Dick, slick and quick, is a wisecracking fellow who may become quite a person when he grows older. Give him and Werbicki time and they will make the grade to success.

Oh yes, and Landry—good, old, dimwitted Landry—is the information bureau in person. He is a kid who has lots to learn and has little time in which to accomplish this deed and a darn good guy if I must say so. I can't make Banelman out. For a fellow with a college education, he is hurting. Sure, he is well read, but he does lack simple common sense. At times, I find him rather thoughtless and neglectful. It appears to me that the wrong people have the advantage of a good education.

I know these boys too well. I sleep with them, I eat with them, and we traveled far and wide, encountering many dangerous incidents together. I like my boys. They have worked well for me. Never once did any give me the least bit of trouble. Never once did any of them hesitate to perform his duty, whether under fire, bad weather, or lack of sleep and food. We worked as a team.

When Mock left the section, I lost a good man. Mock kept me humored and amused with his political views. Mock is a radical one in a way that isn't helping him much. Boyte isn't with the section anymore either. He was an individualist, a good, clean soldier, and a darn good cook. He cooked our rabbits in Geilenkirchen. Even Captain Chrisman liked the rabbit dinner.

I remember so much. Some days were lousy, and some were hard. But almost every day endangered our lives. We all had close calls. Some of our friends are gone forever. Some have been wounded. All in all, we are still a family with our good moments and our bad moments. Such is life.

Hindenburg
May 1, 1945

A news flash came over the air a few moments ago that Hitler is dead. He was an enemy to millions of us who have never seen him personally and no doubt never will see his corpse, and he affected the personal progress and ambitions of each of us. Coincidentally, I am billeted in a village named Hindenburg, the namesake of the man who made Hitler his successor to the Reich. Can this mean the climax of a long and hard-fought war? Have the leaders of this war accomplished their missions? Roosevelt, Hitler, and Mussolini, the leaders of World War II, have left the battlegrounds, only to find compensation and a peace of heart and mind in another world. May God have mercy on their souls, for all world leaders have their good as well as bad ideas and principles.

In this confusing and bewildering world, a man asks so many questions, and it is difficult to give the correct answer. The war, for instance, in reaching its final climax, will no doubt find all responsible leaders dead. The war is progressing in a jumbled fashion. Rumors, rumors, and rumors are flying. Searching for the purpose of this grueling war leaves one in a state of complete confusion as it comes to a climax. Who will be punished for this conflict? What has been gained? Who was right or wrong? The good and the bad are both dead today. Life is so limited, and yet mankind tries so hard to reach entirely too far beyond its goal, only to go crumbling down. Men are such fools, such darn stupid fools.

Apenburg
May 9, 1945

We are now troops of occupation. Once again we have the disgusting routine of garrison training. How long we shall stay here is hard to guess. We are low on the priority list for the China Burma India Theater. Garrison life is dull, and so from here on, I will relate very little except on special occasions. The ending of this war has brought my book to a climax, if a very dull one. I am only thankful I was able to finish a synopsis of my everyday occurrences during these heydays of the battle of Germany.

Hanover
May 19, 1945

Several days have gone by since my departure from Apenburg. Saying *auf Wiedersehen* to those with whom I have made friends was a most difficult ordeal. I shall never forget my friends of Apenburg. In peace and in war, I shall always remember them. Auf Wiedersehen, my Fraulein, whom I so secretly hold dear to my heart.

Bruggen
May 26, 1945

Many incidents have passed my way since Victory in Europe Day. Some I have forgotten, and some I may never forget.

For one week, I was in charge of a guard detail patrolling a soldiers' hospital consisting of former Schutzstaffel troops, the flower of the German army. I have now returned to the chateau. I can't make myself accustomed to the quiet and dull routine of garrison. I feel lost and I am tired. I think of the past several months and what has all this led to.

Hamelin
May 28, 1945

Gronau and Bruggen are but more stepping-stones and memories in our long journey toward home.

Once again we have reached the Wessel River. Several weeks ago, the Germans delayed our drive for two days on this very river, putting up stiff resistance. And now, once again, we live in a mansion only fifty yards from the very banks of the Wessel. Peace and serene beauty once again prevail in the Wessel valley.

We left Von Reden's chateau early today, traveling thirty miles to Hamelin, the legendary town of the Pied Piper. We now occupy the home of Von Beckin, a home built by the aristocratic line of the late eighteenth century. The Wessel flows alongside, making a sharp bend. Here is where the beauty of Germany is supreme.

We have been settling into the town for the past week. This has been a complete rest for most of us. I know it has been for me. Times and conditions have changed considerably since the ending of the war. We are strictly GI once again.

We will move in a couple of days, making a long jump of about 250 miles.

Since payday, the boys have been gambling to the wee hours of the morning.

I can't write or say much. Everything seems to have come to a standstill as far as excitements are concerned.

The time is eight thirty in the evening. A good part of the day was chilly and cloudy, and now, with the late evening descending upon us, the sun has come out, casting a shadow against the abundantly flowered courtyard, where children are playing. It is nice to hear the occasional sound of children's voices.

I went swimming yesterday in a most lovely and luxurious pool. It is as nice as the pool in Gronau. The Germans were well up-to-date in their recreation facilities. Most of our training is now devoted to sports and swimming.

We are pulling out early Sunday morning, one step closer to home. It is now definite that we will not be troops of occupation. We are biding our time for shipping space on our homeward return.

Our dog, Spearhead, is certainly growing rapidly. He awoke me this morning by kissing me on the face. I remember the days when he could barely stand on all fours.

We picked him up during the early days of our drive across Germany. He is quite a fellow and has been fraternizing lately. He is breaking one of the strictest of all army disciplinary army regulations. But then, I know a few fellows—fellows who are considered intelligent—taking severe chances of court martial in relation to fraternizing.

Somehow, I can't blame the boys, because the girls in Germany are beautiful and pleasing. And then I must consider the fact we went through six months of continuous combat.

At four o'clock yesterday morning, we left Hamelin, making a long trip of 235 miles through occupied territory of the First Army. Our journey took fifteen hours to complete. We drove on the best roads in Germany, making most of the trip on superhighways, better known as the Autobahn. We went through Paderborn, a fairly large city that was very badly destroyed, and also went through Frankfurt am Main. Despite the resistance the Germans put up at Frankfurt, it wasn't destroyed as extensively as Mannheim, Munster, and Hanover. I made the trip on a weapons carrier with Frank, Charley, Denny, Dick, Ike, Villines, Ballinger, and of course, Spearhead was with us, and at times he was a problem.

We are living in a beautiful little home. The rear view of the home gives us a view of at least fifteen miles of flat, beautiful timberland and orchards.

We are pulling out of here in the morning. The road back has taken us to the southwestern part of Germany. We are near the Rhineland once again. The more I see of Germany, the more I am inclined to believe these people had a wonderful standard of living. I am sure most of my friends will agree that Germany is a beautiful, prosperous, and progressive nation. The people of Germany were all fools to plunge into a long and bitter war, for they are the cause of the destruction of a picturesque and colorful nation.

Ansbach
June 12, 1945

We moved south about thirty miles, arriving in this small village a little before noon. Going through Heidelberg (famous for its university), we crossed to the south bank of the Neckar River. For a moment, I thought we had crossed the Rhine. We rode the bank of this river for at least ten miles. This river runs deep in a valley. We are now in the high hills of southern Germany.

Our present accommodations are not much to speak of. We must consider that this is a very old village. Most of the inhabitants are made up of children and oldsters.

Ansbach
June 13, 1945

I'm ready to go home. This moving around from sector to sector is becoming very monotonous. We aren't doing anything that is worthwhile to consider. We are merely killing time. At one point, I did have a group set up at Enschede and Gronau, but that is now something of the past.

We have had plenty of rain for the past two days.

We drove back to Weinheim this morning to attend a Railsplitter Society meeting at the Apollo-Theatre. The society is progressing slowly but firmly.

I'm going on pass in the morning to Heidelberg. I've been through the town several times, but this is my first opportunity to visit for a few hours.

Dick is my roommate. He is a darn good fellow to have around. I've nicknamed him the good-humor man. Dick and I have shared rooms on several occasions, and together, we manage to keep our quarters clean and comfortable.

I've been on a fourteen-hour pass today to Heidelberg. Throughout the entire war, Heidelberg has been declared an open city, and due to that agreement between the nations, it is still a very much preserved and cultural place.

The only prevailing destruction is the blown-out bridges connecting the north and south banks of the city.

I revisited Heidelberg this afternoon and went up to see the old castle whose construction first began back in the 1200s. It is situated high on a hilltop overlooking old and new Heidelberg. The scenery at this structure is beautiful. I can see at least twenty-five miles of the surrounding countryside.

Four years ago this morning, I was nervously preparing to take the eventual steps that most men take sooner or later during the span of life. I was to take myself a most wonderful and lovely little girl for my wife. We were then only twenty-four years old. We had wonderful plans. She was so sweet and lovely, adorned in her virgin-white gown of crepe and satin. I would give most anything to relive the memory of walking down the aisle with my wife, Sophie, once more. It happens only once in a lifetime.

We are so many miles apart; however, I am sincerely sure Sophie shall be thinking of me, especially today. I love the dear girl that she is. Sophie, my dear, may your memory of our day always be relived with the eyeglasses of youth.

Another weekend has gone by. In Germany, the people actually make Sunday a legal holiday. During the weekdays, the children in the village run around barefooted, but on Sundays, they dress in their very best.

I went swimming this afternoon, and I believe I threw my arm out of joint in making a dive.

This deployment system is taking a few of the boys away from us. More power to them. Jarret, Hall, Boyte, Fry, Funk, Muslene, Hoover, Reynolds, Thomashefsky, Hewitt, Hanks, Lineham, Nole, Crosby, and Pete have gone. When they will arrive home is hard to say, but it's a good consolation that they are going home at all.

The morning sun is shadowed by heavy, rolling white clouds. An occasional glimpse of blue sky can be seen through broken clouds. The air is chilly from the continuous showers of the day before.

During our two-week stay in this village, I have seen quite a bit of the surrounding area. I paid a visit once to Mosbach to see a United Service Organizations show, went on pass to Heidelberg, and went swimming in Sinsheim.

The boys have been behaving very well. Everyone is on the ball. Our quarters aren't first-class; however, I can say they are fair.

If the beauty of Germany depends upon the souls of German women, I can't see how this feat has been accomplished. To me, the souls and bodies of the German women are most disgusting and degrading. I feel there isn't a woman in Germany who has a sense of belonging, trust, and devotion to any one man.

I can't blame Hitler for never marrying a German woman, for if I possessed his power, I would seek a wife who possessed the virtuous cleanliness of a lily untouched by the filth and insinuations of the human hand.

Although I do not possess Hitler's former power, I have found great love and devotion and also a deep understanding in my wife. To me, my wife is the dearest creation in perfect and lovely womanhood. I am a fortunate man, a very fortunate man.

This is like the old days when we were dashing across Germany. We are living somewhat in class once again. Dick and I share a cozy little den. The room is not large. We sleep on a large davenport with a radio at our heads and a large bay window as the wall. We also have a tiny kitchenette. Two soft easy chairs also tend to make our nook look like the combination of a bedroom and a parlor.

The people in this village appear to be much better off than the people of Ansbach. We left Ansbach early this evening and traveled at least thirty miles. This village is a picturesque and quaint place. It is no larger than Ansbach.

Dick and I have palled up once again. Our days of looting are over, but I see Dick still can't get out of the habit. The music is sweet.

Dick and I have the comfort and convenience of a couple of young schoolboys. I don't know where Dick found the boys' pajamas, but he is wearing them tonight. He's quite a character. Speaking of lounging around and taking it easy, that's exactly what we are doing now. The radio is playing, and we have soft lights to add to a bit of contentment to our relaxed laziness. I think of the Bulge and wonder if all this can be true.

In three days, I have acquainted myself with the village quite well. This village is built around an orchard. Cows are grazing and lazily lolling about. The village church is of the Catholic faith and was built in 1809. The homes are nice, some built in modern design but most painted or color-washed in blue, green, purple, and white. Many windowsills have a display of various species of potted flowers. The village in itself is colorful and harmonious. The people are friendly.

I'm taking another trip to Heidelberg in the morning. The Fourth of July is a legal holiday throughout.

The world comes to a complete standstill in this quaint village of Limbach. The evening is beautiful and serene, except for an occasional voice or the sound of a pounding axe. Only the perpetual chirping of birds in the distance can be heard continuously.

I spent the Fourth of July in Heidelberg. This is my third visit to this cultural town, and I have fallen in love with it. It is a city of luxurious apartment houses and shady, cool avenues. Heidelberg is a city of trees and flowers. The people of Heidelberg are flashy and well learned. I met several Germans who speak English excellently.

We held our first retreat parade today since we left Camp Claiborne. We marched on the fields of clover, the steady tramping of feet creating a dizzy and sweet aroma.

In the early spring, the apple blooms added a wonderful and colorful bit of beauty to an ugly war. With the ending of the war, the fields, orchards, and pastures added the flaming red of the blooming poppies and the picturesque and colorful contrast of the fields of clover and buttercups. Now it is tulip time in Germany.

Limbach
July 12, 1945

My activities for the past five days have been varied. On Monday, I went to Mannheim for the ball game between the Eighty-Fourth and Sixty-Third Divisions. On Tuesday I devoted the day to swimming. (My arm still pains when I dive.) Wednesday evening, I went to see "Rhapsody in Blue"; (The music was wonderful.) Earlier in the evening, I visited friends to drink some wine.

Today, I went to Weinheim once again to attend a Railsplitters meeting. The meeting was short, and I was back in Heidelberg before dinner. I spent the day and evening in Heidelberg, and during the evening, I saw a division boxing meet.

Heidelberg is my second home. This wonderful city has taught me that there is sympathy and understanding, there is a feeling of love, there is a feeling of not wanting to hate, and beauty and youth are very much alive. Heidelberg has taught me all this. Heidelberg is the tree of paradise in all its colorful beauty. Heidelberg is a symphony that reaches a high octave of melodious music.

The Heidelberg Stadium is perched high atop a five-hundred-foot hill overlooking the Neckar River. Actually, it is a concert bowl with a capacity of ten thousand people. The breeze is cool atop this hill, bringing with it a sweet scent of lavender.

Limbach
2400
July 16, 1945

During the past week, Mom has enjoyed the company of Broggy Johnson and myself. Visiting Mom's home was always a welcoming sign for a pleasant evening.

I have been drinking too much lately. I must stop.

Tonight, for the first time, Dick has gone to bed early in the evening.

I must get away from Limbach for a few days. I don't like the way things are turning out.

We have had much rain today. It rained continuously until late in the evening.

I have been visiting Mom's home quite often lately. She told me yesterday evening that this is the first time she has laughed and had so much fun in the last six years.

I would like to take a pass to Heidelberg. I went back to Lindenberg this noon to see the Eighty-Fourth win the swimming meet against other contestants in the Seventh Army. I would like to have hopped off at Heidelberg but did not have the opportunity.

Mom gave me a bunch of freshly cut carnations to refresh my quarters.

I have performed many duties in the army; however, one of the most difficult for me was to search civilian homes for contraband. On the first morning of our search, we had taken over Mosbach. It is quite an experience searching people's homes. None of the civilians were in the least offended. In fact, all were very cooperative. As the day wore on, it became apparently very silly to search homes of people who were so willing to cooperate.

We have been in Limbach for twenty-six days, and during that period, I have made acquaintances here and in the surrounding valleys. Occasionally, I see a Russian family in Brombach. I also have friends in Trienz and Fahrenboch, not to mention those I have met in Heidelberg. It is an open house when I visit Mom.

The evening is warm and quiet. For the past week, I have been building a target range. I should be finished with it in about two days. If I get the darn thing manipulating as I want it to, I should have a darn good moving target.

I went to Heidelberg with Cliff and Chumley the other day, and as always, I spent a most delightful day there.

Mom insists that Broggy, Johnnie and myself come over tonight for cake and coffee.

Bill is in my room. I like Bill. He is a darn nice person. Bill is the kind of a man you can call a true friend, a friend so rare in this world.

Days come and go, and with the passing of each day, memories pile upon memories. Germany and what has happened to me here will be hard to forget. It has been a long road from Geilenkirchen to Limbach.

We have had plenty of rain during the past two days.

The battalion shot the hell out of my targets.

I went to Heidelberg last Tuesday evening. Again, the hours spent in this delightful city were most wonderful. I have found music and poetry in Heidelberg.

I have been staying close to home during the past two days.

Mom asked a favor of me that I knew was useless for me to try and fulfill.

Five days of continuous rainfall brought on a beautifully cool and comfortable weekend. *Alles ist gut.*

Captain Chrisman is becoming very unpopular with the boys.

The news coming from Japan sounds very encouraging.

We had a near tragic experience early yesterday when Villines burned himself severely about his arms with gasoline. Men do too many things carelessly or unthinkingly that usually have terrible consequences.

If I dare say so, I must admit my section has the best-dressed and neatest men in the battery. If the battery as a whole looked upon my men as a good example of cleanliness and neatness, we would then have a shining and meticulous battery.

Dick and I are very proud of our little apartment. Captain Chrisman occasionally casts an envious glance upon our little den.

Early this morning, in this quiet and peaceful little village, the news came over the air that Japan had surrendered. We had not much to rejoice for, because we as combat soldiers understood the true meaning of surrender. It means that a battle is over—a long battle for which both sides paid heavily. It means we do not have to sweat out the coming day, and it gives us the hope that we will live to see the next day and the next day. If we rejoice, we do so only within our hearts, for now we feel that we might relax and sit back and say to ourselves, "We have met and encountered a tough enemy and can thank God that we were just a little bit tougher."

My best wishes to the combat soldiers in the Pacific. They fought a tough and rugged battle.

Limbach
August 20, 1945

The time comes when a man does something that requires some sort of an explanation. What I have done, as far as I am concerned, does not need an explanation.

If my conduct within the past several days was so drastic as to enforce a reduction of my grade, then I can only say that what I did was well worth the price. I realized and fully understood what I was doing, and if I am condemned for being so wrong, then I can only show sympathy for those who passed judgment, because they have not yet have learned how to live and have not yet begun to understand the beautiful significance of human and emotional nature.

Limbach
August 28, 1945

On this beautiful afternoon, I make my conscience feel at ease and think of my past days in Germany. I have lived practically a lifetime in this country. I have witnessed death and destruction. I have been hated and loved, and I have cussed and laughed. My conscience has felt the agony of tenseness and the tenderness of love and companionship. I have seen Germany in all its ugliness, and I have seen Germany in all its supreme beauty and emotional understanding. I share many memories in this country, some ugly and some beautiful. My heart does not belong in Germany. My greatest desire is to leave before I become too deeply involved.

Limbach
August 29, 1945

The road back for the German soldier has been long. He comes back looking tired, haggard, and underfed. His uniform is free of the colorful and conspicuous markings from his heyday as a member of the Hitler Wehrmacht or the famous SS Panzertruppen. He trudges back home without any flag waving or band cheering. He enters town quietly to be greeted casually by his friends. His shoulders are slumped as if offering his apologies for the offenses of the German people.

The German soldier comes home a beaten man, a tired man, a man who probably in his heart feels he is not wanted. The road back is the beginning and the end of the German soldier in defeat.

Two weeks have passed since I became a private once again. During those two weeks, I have done practically nothing. It is not I who has paid the consequences, but my wife and mother. I feel pain that they are disappointed to learn of my present standing.

All is quiet and serene in Limbach. Autumn is making an early appearance. I have high hopes of coming home by Christmas. I have a total of seventy-two points now, which should help me make a trip home shortly.

The battery in general is not a battery anymore. No one seems to care or show any interest. The war has ended, and with that end, a complete lack of enthusiasm has arrived. Our only thoughts now seem to be the desire to get the hell out of this damned army and come home.

A Tribute to Heidelberg

I know Heidelberg, and Heidelberg knows me. This picturesque and beautiful city is alive with music and poetry. It has culture and vitality. The people here would rather sing and dance than eat. Heidelberg is romance, and it is rich emotionally. The people here are as I am—trying to enjoy life the best way they know how. We are such damned idiots. We are emotionally carried away by dreams and fantasies. Heidelberg is the symphony of music between heaven and earth.

We rave and shout of the atrocities and barbarism of the Nazis. Yesterday, for the first time, I found out how stupid and low-down our staff can be. There is a reason and a cause for all happenings and incidents, but yesterday's incident was uncalled for in the manner in which it was executed.

For the past month, the Counter Intelligence Corps has been suspicious of a particular village. Four times in the past, it had been ransacked without any good results. Yesterday, we were called upon once again to make a thorough job. Hay and wheat that recently had been stored in the barns were literally thrown outside, exposed to threatening weather. This is their winter food. Neatly piled wood stocks were deliberately torn down. A very fine example we have shown these people.

C Battery isn't an organization any more. We are merely a group of civilians waiting for our turn to come home. Discipline is something of the past. As hard as the battery captain may try to reorganize his battery, he has lost complete control of the men. Many of my friends have left, and many more will leave in a few days.

I am going to Mannheim in the morning to attend a meeting. Maybe, if the opportunity arises, I will stay in Heidelberg on my way back. For reasons difficult to explain, this beautiful city has become deeply embedded within my heart. It is here that I have found warmth, simplicity, and truthfulness of the heart and mind.

Limbach
September 13, 1945

I am on the last page of my writing, and with this last page has arrived a surprising order, bringing my stay here in Germany to the beginning of its end.

I am told I will start moving Saturday. This sudden alertness threw me off balance. I was not prepared, and what present plans I had made no doubt must be forgotten.

Mom says for my sake she is happy to hear that I am going home, but she will miss me very much. I know she has become very fond of me. We have had many laughs in this old house.

Limbach
September 14, 1945

Seven and a half months ago today, I made my first entry in this book. I did not know what the future had in store for me. We had it pretty rough in those days, and it was only the beginning of the end.

Today, I make my last entry and will possibly spend my last day in Limbach. I am packed and ready to pull out. Many sentiments and memories make an appearance within a man's heart and brain. In Germany, I shall recall many pleasant moments, as well as many moments of anguish and disappointment. Sometimes a man lives a lifetime in a matter of a few months. Such is the will of destiny.

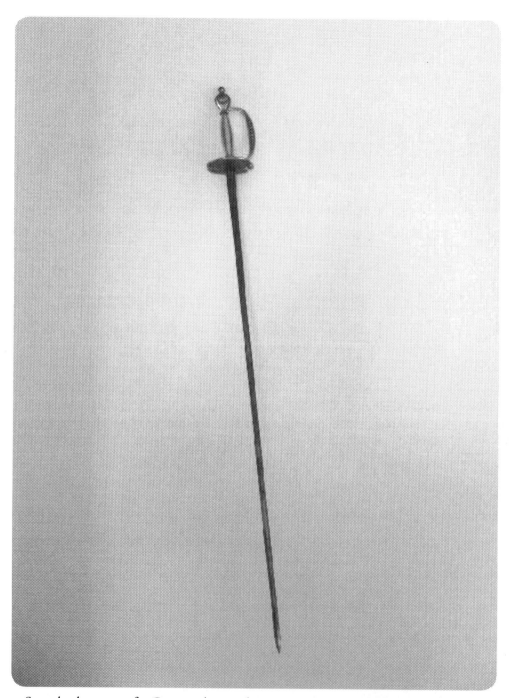

Sword taken out of a German house that was once occupied by the Germans.

CERTIFICATE

Sept 27 1945
(Date)

1. I certify that I have personally examined the items of captured enemy equipment in the possession of _Pvt Frank Pappas_ and that the bearer is officially authorized by the Theater Commander, under the provisions of Sec VI, Cir 155, WD, 28 May 1945, to retain as his personal property the articles listed in Par 3, below.

2. I further certify that if such items are to be mailed to the US, they do not include any items prohibited by Sec VI, Cir 155, WD, 28 May 1945.

3. The items referred to are : One German pistol P-38
Cal, 9m #7203

James W Richard C
(Signature)

1st LT 535 FA BH
(Rank, Branch and Organization)

(This certificate will be prepared in duplicate)

AG USFET Form N° 32

Lot. 5-46 5,000,000 78,920

Capture paper for gun

75

Gun taken out of a pill box on the Siegfried Line

German gun - P.38. Ser# 7203-R

Customs paper for taking home gun

Frank Pappas is the person on the left.

Picture of Sophie Pappas (wife), Frank Pappas (know as Sonny), and Sergeant Frank Pappas.

327th Field Artillery photo of C Battery.

Picture of original journals.

Printed in the United States
By Bookmasters